NONFICTION PASSAGES

With
Graphic
Organizers
for
Independent Practice

by Alice Boynton and Wiley Blevins

NEW YORK • TORONTO • LONDON • AUCKLAND • SYDNEY
MEXICO CITY • NEW DELHI • HONG KONG • BUENOS AIRES

Teaching
Resources

TEXT CREDITS: Joke from LITTLE GIANT BOOK OF SCHOOL JOKES edited by Charles Keller, published by Sterling Publishing Co. Copyright © 2000 by Charles Keller. Reprinted by permission. "Get a Kick Out of Martial Arts" and "Sequoyah and the Cherokee" from REGIONS: ADVENTURES IN TIME AND PLACE. Copyright © 1997 Macmillan/McGraw Hill. Reprinted by permission. "Nancy Ward: Revolutionary War Leader" reprinted from HEROINES OF THE AMERICAN REVOLUTION by Diane Silcox-Jarrett. Copyright © 1998 by Green Angel Press. Reprinted by permission of Green Angel Press. "What's Buried at Pompeii?" reprinted by permission of www.eyewitnesstohistory.com. "Living on a Jet Plane" "Suited for Survival" "I Was a Scientist in the Rain Forest!" "Beastly Bugs or Cool Critters?" "Change of Heart" "Nature's Neat Noses" "Landslide Disaster!" "Mister Mom" are reprinted from SUPERSCIENCE. Copyright © 1998, 1999, 2001, 2002, 2003 by Scholastic Inc. Reprinted by permission. "Dino-mite Discoveries" "Robot Coming Through" "A Dog's Life" "Freedom's Trail" "Hope for Orangutans" "Twister!" "It's About Time!" "Monarchs Take Flight" "Breaking Barriers" "At the Bottom of the World" are reprinted from SCHOLASTIC NEWS. Copyright © 1999, 2002, 2003 by Scholastic Inc. Reprinted by permission. "Calling America Home" and "Celebrate Hispanic Heritage" are reprinted from www.scholastic.com. Copyright © 2004 by Scholastic Inc. Reprinted by permission. "Heart Thumping Workouts" by Bob Hugel from SCHOLASTIC CHOICES magazine, January 1999. Copyright © 1999 by Scholastic Inc. All rights reserved. "From Pampas to Patagonia: South America" from A FIRST ATLAS. Copyright © 1995 by Scholastic Inc. & Two-Can Publishing Ltd. Reprinted by permission.

PHOTO CREDITS (INTERIOR): Title page: (clockwise from top left): Scholastic archive, Library of Congress, Courtesy of Independence National Historic Park via SODA; Laura Hamilton/National Science Foundation, Scholastic Photo Archive, Ana Esperanza Nance/SODA, Courtesy of Honda, Photodisc via SODA; Page 9: Will McIntyre/Getty Images; Page 12: Courtesy of NASA; Page 15: (left) Handout/Reuters/Corbis Images, (right) Ohio State University/Getty Images/Newscom, (bottom) AFP/Newscom; Page 18: Courtesy of Honda; Page 21: (top left) Courtesy of Independence National Historic Park via SODA, (top center left) North Wind Picture Archives, (top center right) Bettmann/Corbis Images, (bottom center) Courtesy of the Navy, (bottom right) The New York Public Library via Scholastic Photo Archives; Page 24: (top left) Lenny Ignelzi/AP Wide World Photos, (center) Mapman via Scholastic Magazine Archives, (bottom) Chris Collins/Corbis Images; Page 27: North Wind Picture Archives; Page 28: (center) Library of Congress, (bottom) Bettmann/Corbis Images; Page 31: Joseph Sohm/Visions of America/Corbis Images; Page 32: Mapman/SODA; Page 35: Theo Allofs/Corbis Images; Page 36: (top left) Gerry Ellis / Minden Pictures, (center right) Mapman via Scholastic Magazine Archives; Page 39: (top) Lawrence M. Sawyer/Photodisc/Getty Images; Page 42: Mapman via Scholastic Magazine Archives; Page 43: Eve Nilson; Page 44: (top) Michael & Patricia Fogden/Corbis Images, (bottom) Kevin Schafer/The Image Bank/Getty Images; Page 47: Scholastic archive; Page 50: Thinkstock/PictureQuest; Page 51: Photodisc/PictureQuest; Page 54: (top) Kit Houghton/Corbis Images, (bottom) Mapman via SODA; Page 55: (top) Richard I'Anson/Lonely Planet Images; Page 58: (left) Wild Pictures/Alamy; (right) Robert & Linda Mitchell; Page 59: (top) Ana Esperanza Nance/SODA, (bottom) Thomas Eisner; Page 60: Photodisc via SODA; Page 61: (top) Robert & Linda Mitchell, (center) Thomas Eisner, (bottom) Wild Pictures/Alamy; Page 62: (right) North Wind Picture Archives; Page 63: Photograph by William Ross Mills/tiro.com; Page 64: The Granger Collection, New York; Page 67: Greg Harlin/Frank H. McClung Museum; Page 71 (left) Wally McNamee/Corbis, (right) Tom Brakefield/DigitalVision; Page 72: (center left) Creatas/PictureQuest, (center right) Corbis Images/PictureQuest, (bottom right) Thomas Brummett/ Photodisc/ PictureQuest; Page 75: (left) Gavriel Jecan/Corbis Images, (right) Alan & Linda Detrick / Photo Researchers, Inc.; Page 76: (top) Tom Brakefield/DigitalVision, (bottom) Michael & Patricia Fogden; Page 79: Rusty Russell/Getty Images; Page 83: (center) Bettmann/Corbis Images, (bottom) Lambert/Getty Images; Page 84: (left) Creatas/PictureQuest, (right) Supreme Court via SODA; Page 87: Paul Sakuma/AP Wide World Photo; Page 89: La Prensa Grafica/AP Wide World Photo; Page 92: The Granger Collection, New York; Page 93: part of the monument to Biddy Mason, Los Angeles, photo courtesy of Ruth Wallach, USC; Page 96: Franklin Viola/Animals Animals; Page 97: (top) George Grall/National Geographic Image Collection, (bottom) Rudy Kuiter/OSF/Animals Animals; Page 100: Photodisc via SODA; Page 101: (top) Danny Lehman/Corbis Images, (bottom) Mapman via Scholastic Magazine Archive; Page 103: Mapman via Scholastic Magazine Archive; Page 104: (center) Archive Photos/Getty Images, (bottom) David Butow/Corbis SABA; Page 105: (top) AP Wide World Photos, (center) Scholastic Photo Archive, (bottom) NASA/Stock Boston, Inc./PictureQuest; Page 106: (top) Lenny Ignelzi/AP Wide World Photos, (center) David Atlas/Retna Ltd., (bottom) NASA; Page 109-110: Royalty-Free/Corbis Images; Page 113: AP World Wide Photo; Page 114: (top) Bettmann/Corbis Images, (center) AP Wide World Photo; Page 117: (top) Mapman via Scholastic Magazine Archives, (bottom) Lucia Simion/Peter Arnold Inc; Page 118: (top) Jeffrey Kietzmann/National Science Foundation, (center) Kris Kuenning/National Science Foundation, (bottom) Laura Hamilton/National Science Foundation; Page 119: (top) Kristan Hutchison/National Science Foundation, (center) Bruno P. Zehnder/Peter Arnold Inc., (bottom) David Tipling/Image State/Alamy; Page 122: Massimo Listri/Corbis Images; Page 123: Bettmann/Corbis Images; Page 124: Corbis Images. Photo Editor: Sarah-Maria Vischer-Masino

PHOTO CREDITS (COVER): Mountain, Gorilla, Butterfly, Basketball game: Photodisc via SODA; Dog: Stanley Bach/SODA; Soldiers/Civil War: U.S. Army via SODA; Clouds: David Franck via SODA; Badlands: Badlands National Park via SODA; Rain forest: Digital Vision via SODA; Pompeii: Photodisc Green/Getty Images; Inline skater: The Image Bank/Getty Images; Tornado, Astronaut, Robot arm: Photodisc Red/Getty Images. Photo Editor: Sarah Longacre

Every effort has been made to acquire permission to use the materials in this book. At the time this book went to press the Web site references were current.

Cover design by Maria Lilja
Interior illustration by Mike Moran
Interior design by Melinda Belter

ISBN 0-439-59019-1
Copyright © 2004 by Alice Boynton and Wiley Blevins. All rights reserved.
Printed in the U.S.A.

Contents

Introduction

Teacher trying to teach about magnets . . .

Is there any one of us who hasn't experienced the challenge of teaching nonfiction? A lesson on the circulatory system can cause heartburn; a lesson on tornadoes can leave your head spinning! But we ourselves have always loved reading nonfiction, so we're always searching for engaging ways to turn our students on to the wonders of the world. What we've discovered is that many of our students share our enthusiasm for this genre. This has encouraged us to include more nonfiction in our reading curriculum. That's why we created *Nonfiction Passages With Graphic Organizers for Independent Practice Grades: 4 and up.* The nonfiction passages in this book:

- provide easily-graded, purposeful homework practice correlated to your content area curriculum.

- help you communicate to parents their child's growing reading skills and content area knowledge.

- support both your reading and content area curriculum.

- provide an inexpensive and instant way to increase the amount of nonfiction students read each week.

- are a natural extension of students' reading, science, and social studies class work, not just busy work for homework.

We hope you and your students enjoy the book!

Alice Boynton   Wiley B

Why Is Nonfiction Important?

Of the three types of text required in reading curricula—narrative, expository, and functional—many students lack enough successful experiences with expository (nonfiction) text. Part of the problem may be that they don't have the tools to navigate nonfiction and extract meaning from it. Some researchers have even suggested that the "fourth-grade slump" experienced by many students might be lessened if these children were exposed to more nonfiction in the elementary grades (Chall, Jacobs, and Baldwin, 1990; Duke, 2000). This includes not only having more nonfiction books in the classroom, but also being taught the tools to gain access to the information they contain. Interestingly, recent research has confirmed that some students actually prefer this type of text, so we see the motivation already exists. This certainly is one reason why nonfiction is important in the elementary grades. Other reasons include:

✔ **The ability to understand and write nonfiction is essential for school achievement.** Students encounter increasing amounts of nonfiction as they move through the grades. Their ability to find their way through the multiple features of this text and comprehend it is critical to reading progress.

✔ **High-stakes tests contain loads of nonfiction.** Recent standardized tests that affect students' promotion, graduation, and college acceptance contain approximately 50% reading tasks with nonfiction.

✔ **Reading nonfiction increases world knowledge and language that students don't have access to in daily conversations.** A student's understanding of the vocabulary in a text is highly correlated to his or her comprehension of that text. In addition, higher levels of background knowledge (acquired through wide reading and classroom discussions) are associated with higher comprehension of texts.

✔ **Understanding nonfiction helps to meet the increasing real-world literacy demands.** Recent NAEP (National Assessment of Educational Progress) studies have shown that high school students are graduating at alarming rates without the basic literacy skills required in today's job market. The 1990 U.S. Department of Labor SCANS report recommended that schools help students develop the workplace competencies necessary for today's job demands. These competencies include the ability to use and obtain information from the Internet. Approximately 96% of the text on the Web is informational (Kamil and Lane, 1998).

✔ **Nonfiction is the preferred reading material of many children.** Many kids in our schools are attracted to nonfiction text. The inclusion of more nonfiction in the curriculum for these "Info-Kids" may improve attitudes toward reading and serve as a catalyst for overall literacy growth (Caswell and Duke, 1998; Palmer and Stewart, 2003).

Characteristics of Nonfiction

One approach to teaching students how to read nonfiction—such as content area textbooks—is to build students' skills in identifying and using the various characteristics found in this type of text. For example:

- learning to **preview** the title, headings, and subheadings in a chapter of social studies text will enable the student to anticipate the main ideas that will be covered.

- knowing how to use **text features** (see a list of these graphic aids below) will allow the reader to take additional meaning from them rather than viewing them as a disruption to the flow of the text. In addition, it will help students integrate this information with that provided by the text.

    The following are common text features students will encounter in their science and social studies textbooks.

Diagrams	**Graphs**
Cycle diagrams	**Maps**
Flow charts	**Time lines**
Online sources	**Primary sources**
Text with multiple features	

- identifying the **text structures**, or organizational pattern within the text, will promote students' understanding and retention. Is the author comparing and contrasting life on the frontier with life in the cities? Is the text describing the physical characteristics of carnivorous dinosaurs?

    Five kinds of text structures, or patterns of organization, are commonly found in informational texts. These include the following:

    Description or listing Provides information, such as facts, characteristics, and attributes about a subject, event, person or concept. This organization is the most common pattern found in textbooks.

    Sequence or time order Presents a series of events that take place in a chronological order. The author traces the sequence or the steps in the process.

    Compare and contrast Points out the likenesses and/or differences between two or more subjects.

    Cause and effect Attempts to explain why something happens; how facts or events (causes) lead to other facts or events (effects). A single cause often has several effects. Also, a single event may have several causes.

    Problem and solution Describes a problem and presents one or more solutions to that problem.

How to Use This Book

Sample Nonfiction Text A range of social studies and science articles reflect content area standards.

Comprehension Check Recall and higher-order thinking questions in standardized test bubble format; some also include constructive response questions requiring students to revisit the text to support their answers.

Graphic Organizer With Writing Prompt A graphic aid helps students organize new learning; a writing prompt extends learning through research, debate, and application of text features.

There are many ways we have used the passages in this book. How *you* use them will depend on your teaching style, student needs, schedule, and local curriculum requirements. Here's one management routine that has worked for us.

STEP 1 Distribute photocopies of the selected article, comprehension questions, and graphic organizer. You may wish to march through the articles in the order presented, or use articles related to topics being covered in your regular science and social studies curriculum. Distribute the article on Monday of each week.

STEP 2 Allow the students the entire week to complete the sequence of the lesson. We suggest the following for students:

Monday: Take home the article, read it, and answer the comprehension questions.

Tuesday: Reread the article and complete the graphic organizer.

Wednesday: Complete the writing assignment that follows the graphic organizer.

Thursday: Read the article and writing assignment to a family member. Have the family member sign the page to acknowledge student's completion of it.

Friday: Return the graphic organizer and writing assignment to you.

STEP 3 Review the answers to the comprehension questions as students grade their own papers. Collect the papers and record students' scores.

Content Area Standards Correlation

Selection Title	Content Area Standard
Living on a Jet Plane	Social Studies: Homes Around the World
Suited for Survival: What's on a Space Suit?	Science: Space
Dino-mite Discoveries	Science: Dinosaurs, Extinction, Fossils
Robot Coming Through	Science: Machines (robotics, electricity)
Ben Franklin: His Place in History	Social Studies: U.S. History, Inventions
A Dog's Life	Science: Animals
Freedom's Trail	Social Studies: U.S. History, Slavery
From Sea to Shining Sea: The United States	Social Studies: U.S. Geography, Map Skills
Hope for Orangutans	Science: Endangered Animals
Get a Kick Out of Martial Arts	Science: Physical Fitness
I Was a Scientist in the Rain Forest!	Social Studies: World Regions and Ecosystems, Conservation
Calling America Home	Social Studies: Immigration
Heart Thumping Workouts	Science: Circulatory System, Health
From Pampas to Patagonia: South America	Social Studies: World Regions and Ecosystems
Beastly Bugs or Cool Critters?	Science: Animal Features
Sequoyah and the Cherokee	Social Studies: U.S. History, Famous Americans, Native American History
Nancy Ward: Revolutionary War Leader	Social Studies: U.S. History, Revolutionary War, Native American History
Change of Heart	Science: Health, Human Body
Nature's Neat Noses	Science: Animal Adaptation
Twister!	Science: Weather
It's About Time! Women's Rights	Social Studies: Equal Rights
Landslide Disaster!	Science: Natural Phenomenon, Weather
Biddy Mason	Social Studies: U.S. History, Famous Americans, African-American History
Mister Mom	Science: Animal Life Cycles
Monarchs Take Flight	Science: Animal Life Cycles / Social Studies: Geography
Celebrate Hispanic Heritage	Social Studies: Famous Americans, U.S. History
Drip, Drop, Drip! The Water Cycle	Science: Weather, Water Cycle
Breaking Barriers	Social Studies: African-American History, Equal Rights, U.S. History
At the Bottom of the World	Social Studies: World Regions and Ecosystems, Explorers
What's Buried at Pompeii?	Science: Volcanoes, Archaeology

Living on a Jet Plane

WHEN AN ICE STORM DESTROYED HER HOME IN 1994, Jo Ann Ussery got a radical idea. Turn a "retired" airplane into a new home!

For $2,000, Ussery saved one **Boeing**-727 body (minus wings and tail) from the scrap heap. She rented a truck to carry the **aluminum** (a kind of metal) plane to the spot in **Benoit**, Mississippi, where her house had stood. After ripping out all but the steering wheels, builders put in a kitchen, living room, and bedroom, and a bathroom complete with **Jacuzzi** in the cockpit.

Why does a plane make a good home? Metal is completely waterproof and aluminum never rusts. The thick metal and round shape make the body strong—storms can't do much damage to this house. Though aluminum is lighter than other metals, airplanes still weigh close to 225,000 kg (500,000 lbs)—way more than the average house. So there's little danger of having a plane blow over.

About six people in the world have had the same idea as Ussery. That's one way to recycle!

WORD WISE

This guide will help you with words in the article that you may not know how to pronounce.

aluminum (uh-LOO-min-um)

Benoit (ben-OYT)

Boeing (BO-ing)

Jacuzzi (juh-KOO-zee)

FIRST CLASS LIVING This airplane now has three bedrooms, a living room, a kitchen, a bathroom—and, of course, plenty of windows.

Living on a Jet Plane

Fill in the circle next to the correct answer.

1. Why did Jo Ann think a plane would make a good home?

  (A) It's very large.

  (B) It's very unusual.

  (C) Bad weather will not damage it.

  (D) She wanted to recycle the plane.

2. *Aluminum* is a _____.

  (A) metal

  (B) kind of airplane

  (C) city in Mississippi

  (D) another name for "ice storm"

3. Another title for this article might be _____.

  (A) "Build It Yourself"

  (B) "A Home in the Air"

  (C) "Bad Weather on the Loose"

  (D) "An Unusual Solution"

4. The article states that a plane makes a good home. Underline or highlight four reasons that are given in the article for this statement.

5. How would you like to live in a recycled plane? Why or why not?

  _____

  _____

  _____

  _____

Common Problem, Uncommon Solution

What problem did Jo Ann Ussery have? What was her solution? Why was it a good one? To answer these questions, fill in the graphic organizer below.

Problem

_____

_____

_____

_____

_____

_____

Solution

_____

_____

_____

_____

_____

_____

_____

_____

Why It Worked

* _____

  _____

* _____

  _____

* _____

  _____

* _____

  _____

WRITING Problems often lead people to come up with creative solutions. Many inventions came about because someone was trying to solve a problem. Research and write about an invention that was a solution to a problem.

Suited for Survival

What's on a Space Suit?

READING TIP

As you read, stop and study the diagram.

• Find the letter A and begin reading the diagram.

• After reading each text bubble, follow the line from the bubble to the photo. Study the photo.

• Then go back to where you left off in the diagram.

On December 7, 1998, astronaut Jerry Ross strolled in space to connect the first two modules of the International Space Station. But first he got dressed for the job. What's he wearing? Check it out!

A
Battery Powered "Headlights"
It's dark in space!

B
Mirror The chest of the suit has information panels that show how much air is left in the tank, and more. Ross can't see the panels. So he moves the mirror until he sees their reflections. Of course, the information is written backwards. Why? Check this out in a mirror:

AIR SUPPLY OK

J
Reflection of the Top of the Space Shuttle
Someone snapped this photo from the shuttle's window—one of the black dots in the center.

C
Many Layers
The suit's many layers of high-tech materials don't let air or heat leak through.

I
Power Tool
The end spins like a drill to turn bolts.

D
Tether
When Ross clips this to the shuttle or module, the stiff material keeps him from floating around.

H
Trash Holder
Inside the square are two sets of bristles, like two hairbrushes stuck face-to-face. Ross's trash stays put between the bristles.

G
Portable Life Support System
This backpack holds Ross's air supply, cooling system, and communications radio.

F
Safety Tether
Ross is clipped to the module here.

E
Jet Pack If his tether breaks, Ross can use this jet pack to fly back to the shuttle.

Suited for Survival
What's on a Space Suit?

Fill in the circle next to the correct answer.

1. Why does the astronaut need headlights in space?

   (A) to drive the space vehicles safely

   (B) to see at night in space

   (C) because it's always dark in space

   (D) to guide the spaceship

2. Why does a space suit have many layers?

   (A) to keep the astronaut warm during the cold nights

   (B) to weigh down the astronaut so he won't float away

   (C) to circulate fresh air from the outside

   (D) to keep in air and prevent heat from leaking out

3. What keeps the astronaut from floating out into space?

   (A) jet pack

   (B) tether

   (C) headlights

   (D) support tank

4. Why does the astronaut need a mirror?

   (A) to see himself and others in space

   (B) to see moving objects that might be coming toward him

   (C) to see the location of the spaceship at all times

   (D) to see the reflection of important information on the suit panels

5. Circle the names of items in the diagram that help the astronaut move.
   Underline the names of items that are similar to items you use on Earth.

Suited for Survival
What's on a Space Suit?

Create your own diagram of a space suit. Add labels and information you learned from the article.

WRITING Find another interesting occupation in which the worker wears a special uniform. This may include a firefighter, surgeon, or plumber. Find a picture of the worker in uniform. Paste the picture onto a sheet of paper. Add labels and information detailing each part of the worker's uniform.

DINO-MITE DISCOVERIES

DINOS IN THE NEWS

DINOSAUR DISCOVERIES CONTINUE TO TEACH US NEW THINGS ABOUT THESE VERY OLD CREATURES. HERE ARE SOME OF THE LATEST DINO FINDS.

Big Discovery

It's not the biggest dinosaur ever found, but it's pretty close. The fossils of a dinosaur called Paralititan (pa-RAL-i-TI-tan) were recently found in Egypt. Experts say it was as big as 15 jumbo elephants, and weighed as much as 7 buses! Paralititan may have been the second-largest dinosaur ever. The largest dinosaur was the Argentinosaurus (ar-jen-TEE-no-SORE-us).

Nose Discovery

Dinosaur expert Lawrence Witmer has revealed that dinosaur nostrils were located lower on the dinosaurs' faces than we had thought. That means all the illustrations of dinosaurs have been wrong!

traditional caudal fleshy nostril

new hypothesis: rostral fleshy nostril

Monster

The skeleton of a "monster crocodile" was found in a desert in Niger. The croc, called Sarcosuchus (SARK-oh-SOOK-us), lived about 110 million years ago and was longer than a school bus. With its huge mouth of more than 100 sharp teeth, it didn't just walk with the dinosaurs—it dined on them!

FACT FILE
Niger

- large, landlocked country in west Africa
- takes its name from the Niger River
- became independent in 1960
- official language is French

Dino-mite Discoveries

Fill in the circle next to the correct answer.

1. Where were the fossils of the Paralititan found?

   Ⓐ United States

   Ⓑ Niger

   Ⓒ Egypt

   Ⓓ China

2. What have recent findings taught us about dinosaurs?

   Ⓐ They were larger than we thought.

   Ⓑ The drawings of their faces are wrong.

   Ⓒ They had lots of teeth.

   Ⓓ They lived all over Africa.

3. Which of the following is larger than a Paralititan?

   Ⓐ 10 large elephants

   Ⓑ 7 school buses

   Ⓒ a Sarcosuchus

   Ⓓ an Argentinosaurus

4. Another word for *dined* is _____ .

   Ⓐ killed

   Ⓑ ate

   Ⓒ slept

   Ⓓ chased

5. List three facts you learned from the article.

   _____

   _____

   _____

Dino-mite Discoveries

1. Draw a picture of a Paralititan.

2. Draw a picture of the number of buses that equal the size of the Paralititan.

3. Circle the correct answer.

Which has more teeth?	*person*	*Sarcosuchus*
Which is larger?	*20 elephants*	*Paralititan*
Where are a dinosaur's nostrils?	*high on the face*	*low on the face*

WRITING Find another recent discovery about dinosaurs. Search the Internet for the latest discoveries. Share your findings with the class.

Robot Coming Through

A Japanese-made robot is wowing kids across America with its fancy moves.

Introducing ASIMO

It has hands, arms, and legs. It can walk up and down stairs. It can recognize people and greet them. It's not a human, but it sure acts like one.

It's ASIMO (A-zee-mo), the world's most advanced robot. ASIMO can respond to simple voice commands, **interpret** certain **gestures**, and recognize faces.

The company that makes ASIMO recently launched a North American tour for the robot. ASIMO will visit schools, museums, and colleges. The company hopes that ASIMO will inspire U.S. students to study **robotics**.

How and Why It Works

ASIMO runs on motors powered by rechargeable batteries. The robot is controlled by a remote computer unit.

One of the robot's special abilities is flexible walking. ASIMO can walk up and down stairs. It can also change directions to avoid bumping into things.

ASIMO was developed to help people, such as aiding the disabled or maybe doing chores around the house. ASIMO cannot yet do those things, but may be able to someday.

Right now, the robot recognizes only Japanese words. When ASIMO is not on tour, it is rented to companies in Japan to work as a greeter. ASIMO is also a guide in a science museum in Japan.

Robot Data: ASIMO is four feet tall and weighs about 115 pounds.

ASIMO's View

- ASIMO has a camera in its head that captures information and uses it. ASIMO can then follow a person or greet someone when he or she approaches. It can also recognize a waving human hand and wave back.

- ASIMO also knows the difference between voices and other sounds. It recognizes when its name is called and turns toward the person calling it.

WORD WISE

gesture (JES-chur) A movement of the hands or head to express a feeling or an idea. *The coach gestured to Ann that it was her turn at bat.*

interpret (in-TUR-prit) To decide what something means. *I interpreted his smile as a sign of welcome.*

robotics (row-BOT-iks) The use of computer-controlled robots to do tasks, especially on an assembly line.

Robot Coming Through

1. What feature makes ASIMO so much more advanced than other robots?

    (A) its size

    (B) its ability to move forward and back

    (C) its ability to walk up and down stairs

    (D) its ability to sit down and stand up

2. What technology makes it possible for ASIMO to do so many special things?

    (A) cameras

    (B) microphones

    (C) computers

    (D) motors

3. The article _____ .

    (A) compares and contrasts different robots

    (B) shows the steps in building the robot

    (C) tells the problems in building ASIMO and how they were solved

    (D) describes how the robot looks and what it can do

4. Look in the article for at least four features that ASIMO and human beings have in common. Underline or highlight them.

5. What you think would be a good use for ASIMO?

    _____

    _____

    _____

ASIMO Word Web

Use the word web below to describe ASIMO's features. Fill in each category with information from the article.

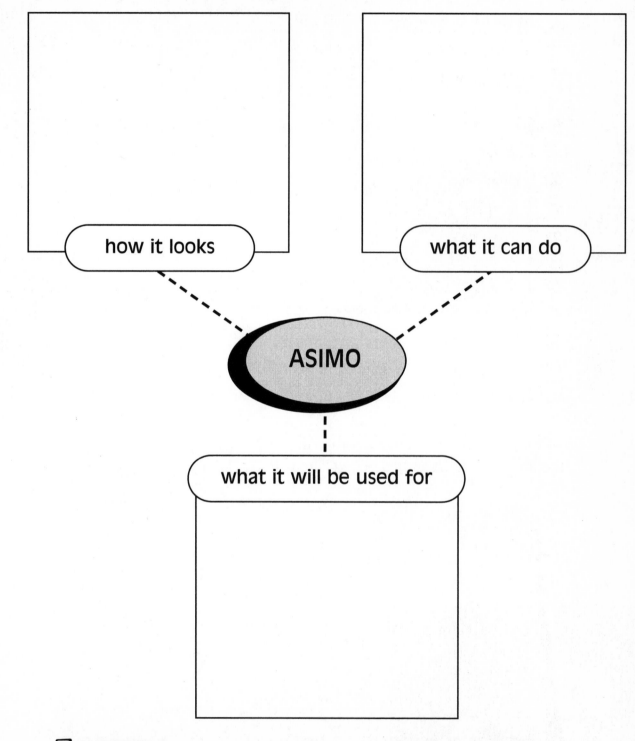

WRITING Write an ad for the amazing ASIMO. Use your graphic organizer to help you describe ASIMO. Choose the features that you think will wow the reader.

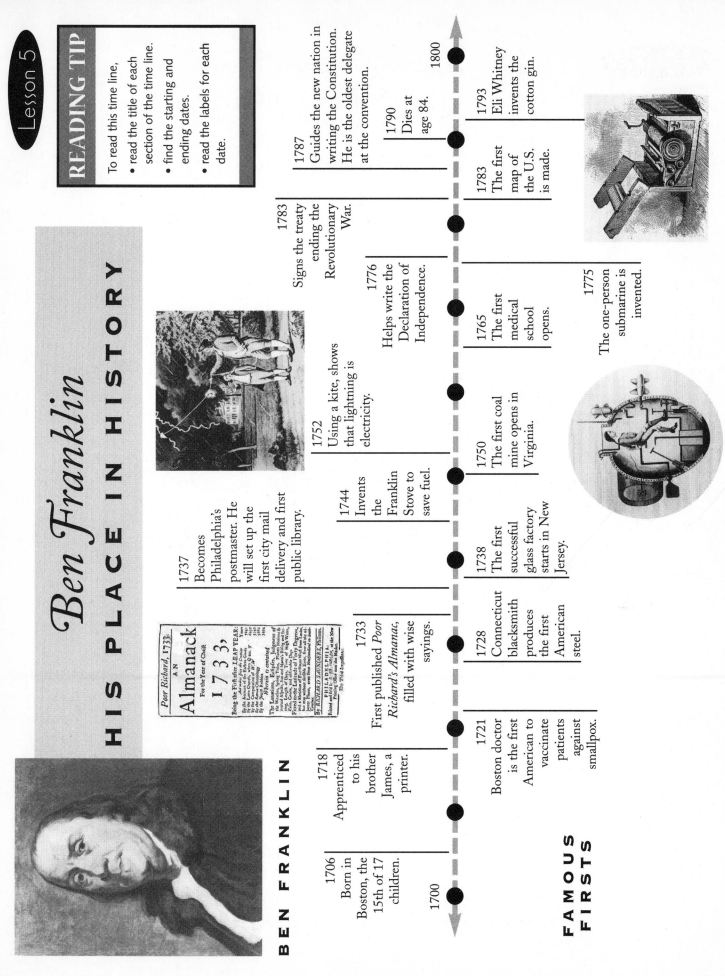

Ben Franklin
HIS PLACE IN HISTORY

BEN FRANKLIN

1706 Born in Boston, the 15th of 17 children.

1718 Apprenticed to his brother James, a printer.

1733 First published *Poor Richard's Almanac*, filled with wise sayings.

1737 Becomes Philadelphia's postmaster. He will set up the first city mail delivery and first public library.

1744 Invents the Franklin Stove to save fuel.

1752 Using a kite, shows that lightning is electricity.

1776 Helps write the Declaration of Independence.

1783 Signs the treaty ending the Revolutionary War.

1787 Guides the new nation in writing the Constitution. He is the oldest delegate at the convention.

1790 Dies at age 84.

1700

1800

FAMOUS FIRSTS

1721 Boston doctor is the first American to vaccinate patients against smallpox.

1728 Connecticut blacksmith produces the first American steel.

1738 The first successful glass factory starts in New Jersey.

1750 The first coal mine opens in Virginia.

1765 The first medical school opens.

1775 The one-person submarine is invented.

1783 The first map of the U.S. is made.

1793 Eli Whitney invents the cotton gin.

Ben Franklin
His Place in History

Fill in the circle next to the correct answer.

1. Which of the following did Ben Franklin <u>not</u> invent or create?

   (A) special stove

   (B) bifocal eyeglasses

   (C) first U.S. public library

   (D) cotton gin

2. Which happened later?

   (A) Ben Franklin publishes *Poor Richard's Almanac.*

   (B) The Declaration of Independence is written.

   (C) The first U.S. coal mine is opened.

   (D) The first one-person submarine is invented.

3. Which word best describes Ben Franklin?

   (A) politician

   (B) inventor

   (C) writer

   (D) all of the above

4. Why was *Poor Richard's Almanac* important?

   (A) It was the first newspaper written in the colonies.

   (B) It ended the Revolutionary War.

   (C) It contained wise sayings and useful information.

   (D) It declared the independence of the U.S.

5. Circle three inventions, discoveries, or events in the time line that affect your life today.

Ben Franklin
His Place in History

Create a time line showing the main events in Ben Franklin's life and a major scientific advance created around that time.

Year	Ben Franklin	Scientific Advance
1718		
1733		
1737		
1752		
1776		
1790		

WRITING Learn more about another famous American who lived during the 1700s. You may wish to research Thomas Jefferson, George Washington, John Adams, Abigail Adams, or Benjamin Banneker. Create a time line showing important events in his or her life.

Dogs are descendants of wolves like the one shown. It's believed that domesticated wolves arrived in the Americas by crossing the Bering Land Bridge. The area is now covered by the Bering Strait. (See map below.)

A Dog's Life
From Wild Wolf to Friendly Fido

By Steph Smith

How does the family dog know from the look on your face that he or she is in the doghouse? Believe it or not, your pooch did not learn from experience. There was no need. A recent study has found that dogs have an inborn talent for reading humans, an ability that may explain why they were one of people's first commonly kept pets.

How Do They Know?

Scientists have known for some time that dogs are **descendants** of wolves. But they didn't know why some wolves were able to be **domesticated**, or tamed to live with or be used by humans.

Researcher Brian Hare says that he has a pretty good idea. He found that dogs outscored both wolves and chimpanzees in tests to see which animal could best read human gestures and facial expressions to find hidden food. The conclusion? Dogs are born with a remarkable ability to read people, making a human-dog relationship very natural.

Humans put dogs to good use, too. They used their new sidekicks to help them hunt, for protection, and for companionship.

Hare believes that wolves developed this people-reading skill as a way of survival. The wolves that became domesticated were the ones that could read humans well enough to find scraps of food. The better those wolves got at reading humans, the more food they found, which increased their chances of survival. Over thousands of years, those wolves turned into today's dogs.

When and Where

Dogs come in more shapes, sizes, and colors than many other animals. Some researchers have recently concluded that the more than 400 breeds of dog come from just a few wolves that roamed East Asia 15,000 years ago.

Domesticated wolves lost some traits because the species didn't need them anymore. For example, they no longer had to hunt down other animals for food. Therefore, they no longer needed large muzzles or big teeth. Over thousands of years, dogs developed that had smaller heads and teeth than their original wolf relatives.

In addition, dogs traveled throughout the world with people and experienced different climates. Dogs living in warmer climates didn't need thick coats, but the ones in colder climates did. Much of today's dog variety comes from breeding. Humans crossbred different kinds of dogs to make even more types of dogs.

ASIA · Bering Strait · NORTH AMERICA · PACIFIC OCEAN

WORD WISE

descendants One's children, their children, and so on.

domesticated An animal tamed so it can live with or be used by humans.

A Dog's Life

Fill in the circle next to the correct answer.

1. Dogs are descendants of what animal?

   (A) hare

   (B) bulldog

   (C) wolf

   (D) dinosaur

2. What can dogs do better than wolves or chimpanzees?

   (A) run faster and farther when in danger

   (B) find food in the wild

   (C) protect their families from attack

   (D) read the expressions on people's faces

3. A *domesticated* animal is _____ .

   (A) wild

   (B) large

   (C) tame

   (D) smart

4. Which statement best describes dogs?

   (A) the world's smartest animal

   (B) a natural human pet

   (C) the most common ancient animal

   (D) the only ancient animal used by humans

5. Underline the sentences that tell why dogs made such great pets.
   Circle the sentences that tell why there are so many types of dogs today.

A Dog's Life

Fill in the Venn diagram below. Record how dogs and wolves are the same and different.

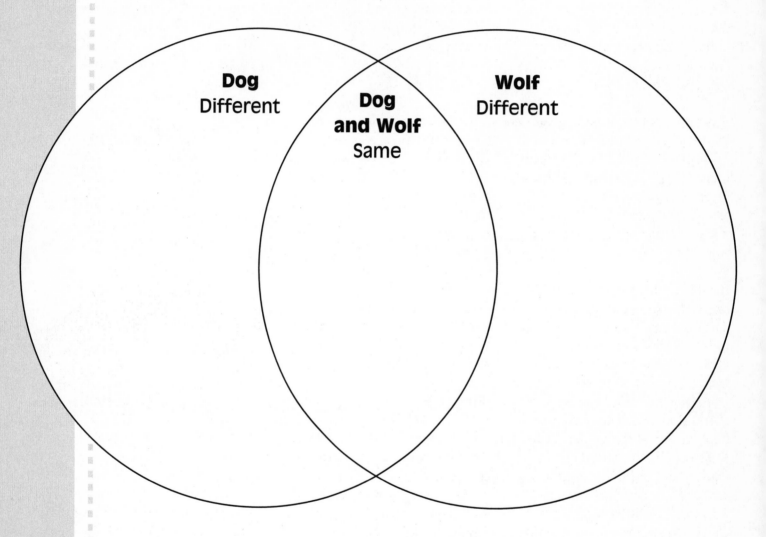

Dog
Different

**Dog
and Wolf**
Same

Wolf
Different

WRITING Find out about another ancient animal, how it was tamed, and how it was used by humans. You may wish to research the history of cats or horses. Record your findings on an illustrated animal time line.

Freedom's Trail

By Dara N. Sharif

The Underground Railroad was neither underground nor a railroad. But its legacy of determination and courage lives on more than a century later.

ANTHONY CORNISH FLED SLAVERY with his dad, mom, and five of his brothers and sisters. The year was 1857. It was a cold and rainy October night. Anthony and his family faced terrible punishment if they were caught. But they were determined to be free. They joined 20 other runaways along the dangerous road to freedom called the Underground Railroad. They traveled more than 100 miles north, from slavery in Cambridge, Maryland, to freedom in Philadelphia, Pennsylvania.

Anthony and his family owed their freedom to the brave men and women of the Underground Railroad. The story of their escape can still be told thanks to the work of William Still, an African-American abolitionist (ab-uh-LISH-uh-nist), who was a major figure of the Underground Railroad. His 1872 book, *The Underground Railroad,* is considered one of the most accurate and detailed descriptions of the secret network of people who risked their lives to free slaves.

Today, Still's love for community and scholarship lives on in his descendants (di-SEND-uhnts), including his great-great-great-grandniece Keaira (kee-AIR-ah) Still, 17, of Lawnside, New Jersey. "Knowing history gives you a sense of pride," says Keaira. "It sets the groundwork for what you want to do with the rest of your life."

A SECRET NETWORK

An abolitionist is someone who worked to end slavery before the Civil War (1861–1865). The Underground Railroad was one of the tools used. The Underground Railroad was neither underground nor a railroad. It was a loose network of people who helped slaves escape. "Conductors" on the road used disguises and secret hiding places to guide their "passengers" to freedom. They often traveled at night with only the light of the North Star to guide them. At each "station," or safe house, "stationmasters" would provide food, shelter, or transportation to the next station.

The danger was great. Slavery was the law in the United States. Runaways could be beaten and returned to slavery. Those who helped them faced jail, fines, even death. Because of this, few people kept detailed records about the Underground Railroad.

WILLIAM STILL

But William Still did keep records. Still was born free in New Jersey in 1821 to parents who had been slaves. He left home to find work in Philadelphia and got a job with the Philadelphia Abolitionist Society. He was named head of the Vigilance Committee, which offered financial help to runaways. This was part of his work on the Underground Railroad.

William Still

Still kept records on everyone who came to him for help. He wanted to let former slaves tell their own stories. He also hoped to help family members who had been separated by slavery find each other again. Still found his own long-lost brother, Peter, while interviewing runaways.

William Still provided runaways with food, clothing, shelter, and contacts for jobs. He found money for their travel farther north. He was arrested many times, but continued despite the risk.

STILL'S LEGACY

One hundred years after Still's death, Keaira says that knowing her family's history gives her a greater sense of responsibility. She gets all A's at school, plays the trombone, and has friends of all races. She hopes to become a psychologist someday. Her life in 21st-century New Jersey is no comparison to the one Anthony Cornish faced as a child on the run from slave catchers. Kids today too often take their freedoms for granted, Keaira says. "I don't think I'd want to think about what life would be like today without my uncle and others like him," she says.

"My ancestors went through much worse," Keaira says. "But they worked through it. If my ancestors could do that, then just think what I can do."

FACT FILE
Underground Railroad

- Conductors were people who helped runaways.
- Stations were hiding places.
- The major destination for runaways was Ontario, Canada.
- Levi Coffin, a Quaker, was called the "president of the Underground Railroad"; he helped over 3,000 slaves escape.

Great Escapes

The Underground Railroad was no longer needed as the U.S. prepared for the Civil War. Slavery was outlawed after the war, in 1865. But it would take another 100 years and the modern civil rights movement headed by Dr. Martin Luther King, Jr. before African-Americans would even begin to see real equality. The railroad was only a step toward freedom. Here are some stories from the road.

MAILED TO FREEDOM: (At top) Henry "Box" Brown hid in a box that was shipped from Virginia to Philadelphia—and freedom.

IN DISGUISE: Ellen Craft disguised herself as a young white man. Her husband, William, pretended to be "his" slave. They rode a real train from Georgia to Philadelphia.

SECRET PASSAGE: John Freeman Walls, who escaped slavery in North Carolina in 1845, included a secret passage behind a fake bookshelf in the house he built in 1846 in Ontario, Canada.

THEIR HERO: (At bottom) Harriet Tubman is pictured with a family that she led out of slavery. Tubman was known as the "Moses of Her People."

Freedom's Trail

Fill in the circle next to the correct answer.

1. Who was William Still?

   (A) a slave

   (B) a writer

   (C) a white abolitionist

   (D) a soldier during the Civil War

2. Which of the following best describes the Underground Railroad?

   (A) a secret train that slaves rode North

   (B) an underground passageway during the Civil War

   (C) a group of people who helped slaves escape to freedom

   (D) a network of conductors and passengers who were against the Civil War

3. Which of these would be <u>your</u> descendant?

   (A) your grandfather

   (B) your mother

   (C) your great-aunt

   (D) your grandson

4. What do Keira and William Still have in common?

   (A) both were slaves

   (B) both worked on the Underground Railroad

   (C) both were writers

   (D) both were affected by slavery

5. List the many ways mentioned in the article that slaves used to escape to freedom.

   _____

   _____

   _____

Freedom's Trail

We learn about historical events from many sources. List the kinds of information learned from these sources. Use examples from the article when appropriate.

Source	Information Learned	Examples
newspapers		
books		
interviews		
letters		
old photographs		
diaries		
monuments		

WRITING Write a story told to you by one of your ancestors, such as a grandparent. Think of an event related to something in history.

From Sea to Shining Sea

★ ★ ★ ★ ★ ★ ★ ★ ★ ★ ★ ★ ★ ★ ★ ★

THE UNITED STATES

★ ★ ★ ★ ★ ★ ★ ★ ★ ★ ★ ★ ★ ★ ★ ★

The United States is divided into 50 states. The United States, except for the state of Hawaii, is part of the continent of North America. Most of the United States lies between the Atlantic Ocean and the Pacific Ocean and is bordered by Canada on the north and Mexico on the south. Alaska is separated from the lower 48 states by Canada. Hawaii is an island group in the Pacific Ocean.

Land of the United States

The United States has two major mountain ranges—the Appalachians in the east and the Rockies in the west. With only a few peaks above 6,000 feet, the Appalachian Mountains are much lower than the Rockies. The Appalachians extend 2,000 miles from northeastern Canada all the way south to Alabama. The Rocky Mountains extend 3,000 miles from northwestern Canada south to Arizona and New Mexico. The highest peak, rising 20,320 feet, is Mount McKinley in Alaska.

The lowest, hottest, and driest part of the United States is Death Valley. Located in southeastern California, Death Valley is 282 feet below sea level.

U.S. Rivers and Lakes

The Mississippi River with its tributaries is the country's largest river system, draining parts of 31 states. The Mississippi flows 2,340 miles from Minnesota to the Gulf of Mexico.

The Great Salt Lake in northern Utah is the largest inland body of salt water in the Western Hemisphere.

FACT FILE
Latitude and Longitude

You can use a grid of imaginary lines on a map to find the exact location or "address" of every place on the earth. Here's how:

- **Latitude lines** run parallel to the equator. They measure in degrees the distance north or south of the equator. The symbol ° stands for degrees.

- **Longitude lines** run from the North Pole to the South Pole. They measure in degrees the distance east or west from the starting place, which is marked 0° on a map.

- The point at which the latitude and longitude lines intersect on a map is the exact address of a place.

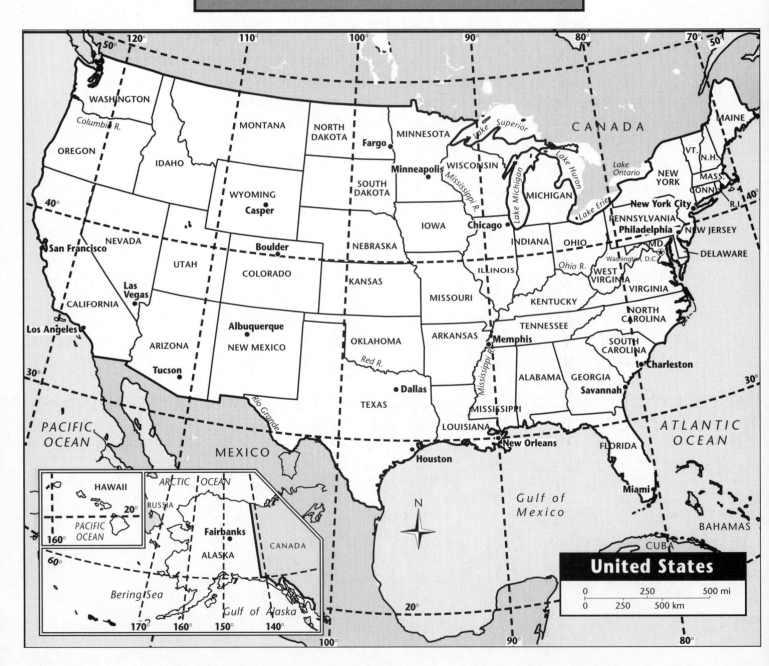

United States

From Sea to Shining Sea

Fill in the circle next to the correct answer.

1. The highest mountain peak is located in _____ .

   (A) Canada

   (B) California

   (C) Alaska

   (D) the Appalachian Mountains

2. Which geographical feature creates a natural boundary line between more than eight states?

   (A) the Rocky Mountains

   (B) Death Valley

   (C) the Appalachian Mountains

   (D) the Mississippi River

3. Which state is <u>not</u> south of Kentucky?

   (A) Indiana

   (B) Georgia

   (C) North Carolina

   (D) Florida

4. Pilots and sailors depend on latitude and longitude to figure out _____ .

   (A) how fast they are going

   (B) exactly where they are at all times

   (C) the weather forecast

   (D) the amount of fuel they have

5. Which city in the U.S. has a latitude of 30° and a longitude of 90°?

   _____

From Sea to Shining Sea

"**From Sea to Shining Sea**" describes geographical features of the United States. **Record some of the features you read about on the graphic organizer below.**

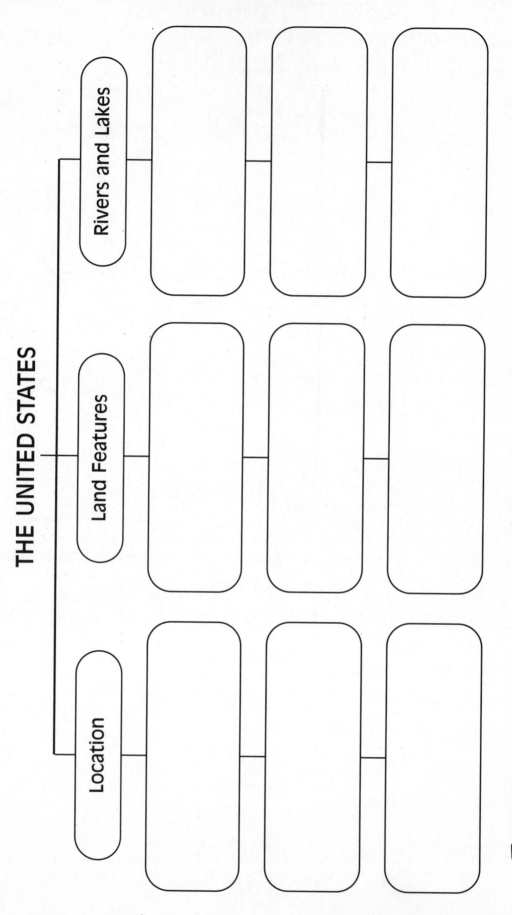

THE UNITED STATES

Location

Land Features

Rivers and Lakes

WRITING Look carefully at the map on page 32. Write five interesting things you observe that were *not* stated in the article. For example, you may notice cities that share the same longitude, states that are on more than one of the Great Lakes, and so on. Be specific. Tell the name of the city or state and the fact that you observe.

HOPE FOR

ORANGUTANS

A newly discovered population of orangutans gives the endangered ape a chance for survival.

By Laura Linn

AN IMPORTANT FIND

Come out, come out, wherever you are! Hidden deep in the rain forests of Borneo in Indonesia, apes with shaggy red hair, oval faces, and deep-set eyes were recently discovered, swinging from tree to tree.

This newfound population of about 2,000 orangutans (uh-RANG-uh-tan) gives a fighting chance to the species for future survival in the wild. Before researchers from the Nature Conservancy stumbled upon the orangutans in East Kalimantan (see map), the ape's future was grim. With the new discovery, the number of known orangutans in the world has increased by 10 percent!

"The find was extremely good news," says Christine Dorsey, a spokesperson for the Nature Conservancy. "There are not many populations of orangutans that have a chance to survive in the wild as this one does."

Orangutan Culture

Orangutans don't have their own music or art, but believe it or not, a new study has found that they do have their own **culture**. To scientists, culture is the ability to learn a new living habit and pass it down to the next generation.

Some orangutans teach their offspring to use sticks to get insects from tree holes. Others say goodnight by blowing out of their closed lips to make a splattering sound.

FACT FILE
About Primates

- Primates are the group of animals that include humans, apes, and monkeys.

- Primates are mammals. They usually give birth to one offspring at a time.

- Primates depend mostly on their vision, not their sense of smell.

- Primates can grasp and hold things well with their hands.

- Primates have large brains in comparison to their body size.

- Primates are social animals. They spend most of their lives in a social group.

◄ *A baby holds on to a stick, which many orangutans use to pick bugs from trees.*

LIFE OF AN ORANGUTAN

Orangutans are among the most endangered **primates** in the world. They live on only two Southeast Asian islands, Sumatra and Borneo. Their numbers have dwindled from more than 300,000 in the early 1900s to about 15,000 today.

Orangutans are the only great apes that live most of their lives in trees. They spend much of their day gracefully swinging from branch to branch in search of food. Fruit, bark, flowers, and insects are some of the favorite snacks of the orangutans. To find and eat their food more easily, some orangutans create tools, such as sticks, to pick insects out of trees.

DISAPPEARING ACT

Orangutans are just one of the 195 different nonhuman species of primates, including gorillas and chimpanzees, that are in danger of becoming **extinct**.

Human activity is the reason these apes are fighting for survival. Habitat loss, due to forest clearing for farming and timber use, continues to be the main threat to the animals. For instance, the forests where orangutans live in the wild are being destroyed for lumber.

Conservationists say that if something is not done to prevent people from cutting down the trees, there won't be any forests left to the orangutans to live in by 2020. Without forests to live in, orangutans have no chance of surviving in the wild.

"Unless extreme action is taken soon, these forests could be gone within the next 10 years, and orangutans along with them," says researcher Birute Galdikas.

Luckily, the newfound group of orangutans has a reasonable chance of survival since they are in a remote area where not much logging has taken place. Their existence offers hope that these creatures will hang on tight and swing freely in the wild for years to come.

Hope for Orangutans

Fill in the circle next to the correct answer.

1. In what part of the world do orangutans live?

   Ⓐ North America

   Ⓑ Australia

   Ⓒ Indonesia

   Ⓓ Africa

2. Which of the animals below are not primates?

   Ⓐ Elephants

   Ⓑ Chimpanzees

   Ⓒ Apes

   Ⓓ Human beings

3. The danger to orangutans is so great because they _____.

   Ⓐ have a small food supply

   Ⓑ live in so few places in the world

   Ⓒ can't adapt to changes in their environment

   Ⓓ have very few offspring

4. Which features outline the main ideas in the text?

   Ⓐ boldfaced words

   Ⓑ photographs and captions

   Ⓒ title and headings

   Ⓓ sidebar

5. Go back to the article. Circle or highlight the causes that explain why orangutans are endangered.

Hope for Orangutans

The text of "Hope for Orangutans" is organized in two ways. Use the file cards below to record the information from each section.

LIFE OF AN ORANGUTAN
Description

Physical _____

_____

Habitat _____

_____

Behavior _____

_____

DISAPPEARING ACT
Cause/Effect

Cause _____

_____

_____

Effect _____

_____

_____

WRITING Which of the statements below do you agree with? Choose a side, and write your opinion. Support your arguments with evidence from the article and other information you know.

* People should be able to farm land that they need for their own and their family's survival.

* We must protect endangered animals because once they are extinct, they are gone forever.

GET A **KICK** OUT OF MARTIAL ARTS

"Yah!" Students shout as loud as thunder as they practice martial arts.

Martial means "warlike," and long ago the martial arts were part of training for war. Today people practice them as sports—for fun, exercise, and self-defense.

The first martial art taught in this country was **kung fu**. It was brought here by Chinese immigrants in the mid-1800s. At first kung fu teachers taught only Chinese Americans. Then in 1964 a teacher in Los Angeles opened his school to everyone. Soon Americans all over the country were learning kung fu.

Immigrants from Asia brought other martial arts. From Japan came **judo**, which means "gentle way," and **karate**. Koreans brought **tae kwan do** (tie-kwon-doe). These sports are a legacy from countries in Asia. They are now enjoyed by millions of Americans.

The boy is competing in kickboxing. He wears special pads to prevent injury.

READING TIP

As you read, stop and study the bar graph.

- Read the title to find out the topic of the graph.

- Look at each label. Think about what the numbers stand for.

- To read the graph, use your finger to trace from the top of the bar to the number on the left.

- Think about the comparisons the graph is making.

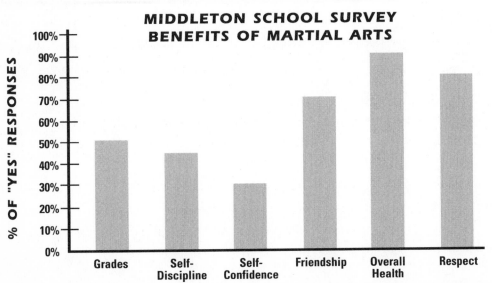

MIDDLETON SCHOOL SURVEY BENEFITS OF MARTIAL ARTS

% OF "YES" RESPONSES

100% / 90% / 80% / 70% / 60% / 50% / 40% / 30% / 20% / 10% / 0%

Grades | Self-Discipline | Self-Confidence | Friendship | Overall Health | Respect

Get a Kick Out of Martial Arts

Fill in the circle next to the correct answer.

1. Which of the following is <u>not</u> a martial art?

   (A) judo

   (B) karate

   (C) wrestling

   (D) tae kwan do

2. What is the biggest benefit of martial arts?

   (A) overall health

   (B) grades

   (C) friendships

   (D) respect

3. In which country did *tae kwan do* begin?

   (A) Taiwan

   (B) Korea

   (C) China

   (D) Japan

4. Why do people practice martial arts?

   (A) fun

   (B) self-defense

   (C) exercise and sport

   (D) all of the above

5. Go back to the article and <u>underline</u> the names of all the martial arts mentioned.

Get a Kick Out of Sports

Take a poll. Ask your classmates what their favorite sport is. Then create a bar graph showing their favorite sports.

Number of Students					
20					
18					
16					
14					
12					
10					
8					
6					
4					
2					

_____ _____ _____ _____ Other

Sports

WRITING Select one type of martial art and learn more about it. Write a brief article about the martial art. Learn one or two moves to show the class.

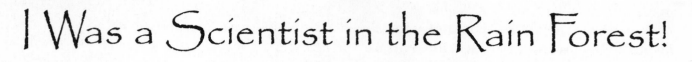
I Was a Scientist in the Rain Forest!

By Eve Nilson

For three months, I worked in one of the most beautiful and threatened places on Earth. Here's some journal entries from my trip.

DAY 1 *Rawp! Rawp! Roar!* I jump awake, thinking I've heard a fire alarm. But then I remember: There's no fire alarm here—I'm in a house deep in a tropical rain forest. After years of dreaming, my wish has come true: I'm living and working in the Brazilian rain forest.

I am 15 years old and will be a junior in high school next fall. For three months, I will work as a field **biologist** studying frogs in the Mata Atlantica, which is Portuguese for Atlantic forest.

Eve Nilson spent three months in the Atlantic Forest on the east coast of Brazil. It's a tropical rain forest, lying between the Tropics of Cancer and Capricorn.

This is one of the most threatened forests in the world. Of the original 8.5 million square kilometers (5.3 million square miles), of Atlantic Forest in Brazil, very little—less than one tenth—remains. The Atlantic Forest is home to 8,567 **species** of plants and animals found nowhere else on Earth. Scientists are working to save this area before these plants and animals disappear forever. The Guapi Acu (GWAP-ee a-SOO) Ecological Reserve, known as REGUA, was established in 1998 to protect the forest.

Last summer, I was lucky to meet Sir Ghillean Prance, a rain forest **botanist**, or plant scientist. Friends had told Sir Ghillean about my interest in the rain forest. He knew that I had spent

WORD WISE

This guide will help you with words in the article that you may not know how to pronounce.

biologist (bi-AHL-uh-jist)

botanist (BOT-uh-nist)

concerto (kuhn-CHAIR-toh)

jaguar (JAG-wahr)

morpho (MOR-foh)

species (SPEE-sheez)

many summers studying whales with my mother, who is a field biologist. After we talked, he invited me to study this forest.

DAY 2

I get out of bed and find a dozen mosquito bites on my lower back. I seem to be the mosquitoes' favorite meal. They're everywhere!

Because much is known about the birds, animals, and plants of this rain forest, I've decided to study the frogs. I'll compare the frogs that live in a pond in an open field with those living in a dark forest pond. REGUA managers would like to reforest the field pond. But first, they want to be certain no unique frog species live there. My census, or count, will help.

DAY 3

Because frogs are nocturnal, or mostly active at night, I'll do my work after dinner. A guide helps me carry a spotlight, flashlight, tape recorder, notebook, and camera to the forest pond. To enter the jungle we must carry the heavy equipment across two slippery logs suspended over a swift stream.

At the pond, I scan the water with the spotlight, searching for pairs of green frog eyes. But the light only reflects red points of light— the eyes of water spiders. I switch on my audio recorder and begin the recording with the date, location, and weather.

There seem to be frogs in every part of the jungle except this pond. Frogs sing high up in the trees, up in the rain forest canopy over-head, but the pond is silent. I wait patiently.

DAY 4

I'll be recording the frogs every other night.

During the day, I explore the area around my house. Everywhere I look there are insects, plants, and animals I've never seen before. Today, I swim in the cool stream by my house. Afterward, I am startled by a sting-ing bite on my heel. I have placed my bare foot directly in a hill of red ants! My leg seems to be

covered by a river of living dirt. I brush the ants away. Suddenly a blue **morpho** butterfly, my favorite, lands in the path.

DAY 6 Tonight, I head to the field pond, walking briskly under a sky filled with stars. The field pond features a **concerto** of frog calls, or vocalizations, much more lively than the pond. The frogs are silent as I shine the spotlight over the pond, but as soon as I click the light off, their chorus resumes. I listen closely and count. Some frogs have deep voices; they sing "what-IP." Other have high-pitched croaks that sound like squeaky wings. It sounds like "EET-eet." In my notebook, I write down how many types of frog calls I hear. Then I make a note of each frog's location, so I can estimate how many individual frogs are present.

DAY 7 In the morning, I listen to the audiotapes I made the night before, checking my notes against what I hear on the tape. Then I hike up the mountain with other researchers and two rangers. At this altitude, there are countless species of birds, and a warm mist fills the air. We come across fresh **jaguar** tracks, some as large as my outstretched hand. This is where the jaguar sleeps during the day, going down the mountain at night to hunt.

We find a group of brown capuchin (KA-puh-shin) monkeys lounging in the canopy. They quickly move into the forest and we follow their sounds. Suddenly we're in a field of spiny palm trees, whose spikes are extremely painful to touch. We carefully move into a clearing, and for the first time since I've come here, I'm frightened. There is trash everywhere and bullet holes in trees. Animal bones litter the ground. The guide explains that this is a poachers' camp. These hunters have come into the forest and illegally killed animals. They treat this as their own trash dump. We gather up the litter quietly and leave. We're all solemn now.

DAY 8 I return to the jungle site. Still no frogs on the pond!

DAY 9 I'm covered in mosquito bites, though I always wear long-sleeved shirts and long pants, even in this hot and steamy weather. Today while hiking, we heard the call of a spot-billed toucanette (TOO-can-ett) and saw a black-throated trogon (TRO-gan), a brilliant green bird with a bill similar to an anteater's snout.

DAY 10 I visit the site during the day. The edge of the pond is muddy, but I capture some frogs in my net. I photograph them, and let them go. I'll take the photographs to the local university so biologists can help me identify them. Tonight, I'll come back with my recorder and notebook.

CONCLUSION

By the end of my stay, I've counted 8 species of frogs and 23 individual frogs in the field site, none in the forest pond. None of the frog species are unique to REGUA—they are all common frogs found throughout Brazil. Allowing the forest to grow over this field will not destroy the habitat of any unique frog species.

I have always wanted to be a biologist and this experience in Brazil confirmed my desire. And, it's given me hope. I had felt that the rain forest destruction would continue ruthlessly, and that I could do nothing to help. But now I know that there are conservation efforts. And, as a result of my study, students from a local university and scientists from a museum are coming to REGUA weekly to study the plants and animals. My visit helped start an ongoing study of this special forest!

I Was a Scientist in the Rain Forest!

Fill in the circle next to the correct answer.

1. Why did Eve Nilson go to the rain forest in Brazil?

   Ⓐ She wanted an exciting vacation.

   Ⓑ She wanted to help her mom study rain forest animals.

   Ⓒ She was concerned about the threatened rain forest animals.

   Ⓓ She was studying to become a biologist.

2. Why was Eve scared on Day 7?

   Ⓐ She was afraid that a jaguar would attack her.

   Ⓑ She knew dangerous poachers were nearby.

   Ⓒ She was being attacked by stinging red ants.

   Ⓓ She realized that no frogs could be found.

3. A *botanist* is someone who studies _____ .

   Ⓐ frogs

   Ⓑ poachers

   Ⓒ plants

   Ⓓ rainforest animals

4. Why was Eve's trip a success?

   Ⓐ She discovered a unique frog species.

   Ⓑ She cut down only a few trees in the rain forest.

   Ⓒ She discovered a new species of butterfly.

   Ⓓ She made sure that no frog species would be destroyed.

5. List everything Eve did to learn more about the rain forest frogs.

   _____

   _____

   _____

I Was a Scientist in the Rain Forest!

PROBLEM

Rain forest animals are being threatened.

Which animals? _____

_____

_____

Why are they in danger? _____

_____

_____

SOLUTION

What is being done to save these animals?

_____

_____

_____

_____

_____

_____

WRITING Find out more about the rain forests around the world. What are people doing to save the rain forests? What plants and animals are in danger? What peoples live in the rain forest? Create a world map showing where rain forests are located and what is being done to save them.

Calling America Home

Meet two young immigrants. Find out why they and their families left their homelands and what it's like to be a newcomer in America.

Name: **Van**
Birthplace: **Thanh My Loi, Vietnam**
Home: **Seattle, Washington**

Name: **Vedron**
Birthplace: **Vogosca, in what was Yugoslavia**
Home: **Paterson, New Jersey**

I was nine years old when I came to the United States. My first day in America was like being in a prison. I didn't have any friends. I didn't speak any English. And it was so cold! I was used to the warm weather in Vietnam. I really wanted to go home.

My family came to the United States for more freedom and so that I could get a better education. Going to school is very expensive in Vietnam. Plus, you don't get that many opportunities there. Here, if you work hard, you can do anything. I'd like to be a pharmacist some day, to help people who are sick. I strive to do well in school so I can succeed.

I remember when I heard that we were leaving Vietnam, I kept thinking: Will it be the same in America? What is the country like? Will I ever make friends there like I have in Vietnam? I was used to riding my bicycle, eating ice cream on hot, sunny days, and playing with my sister and cousins.

Today I love the United States. This is the country where I want to stay for the rest of my life. I would like to go back to Vietnam only to see my older sister. She is married and has children, and she stayed behind. The day we left Vietnam without her, I felt like a part of myself was missing. Except for my sister, I don't even think about Vietnam anymore. America is my home. This is where I should be.

FACT FILE
Becoming a U.S. Citizen

To become an American citizen, a person must

• be at least 18 years old and have lived in the U.S. legally for at least five years.

• not have been involved in certain criminal activities.

• show that he or she can read, write, speak, and understand basic English.

• demonstrate a knowledge of U.S. history and government by taking a test.

My family left Vogosca, which is in Bosnia, when the war started in 1992. My school was closed. Many of the stores closed. The company where my parents worked closed. We heard gunshots. It was very dangerous to live there. So we moved to Serbia. Then my uncle and his wife came to America in 1996. My family followed in November 1997. I was 12 years old.

It is not scary living in New Jersey. I go to school every day, and my parents go to work. Sometimes my friends and I sit and talk in front of my house until nine o'clock in the evening. I have many friends. They are from Mexico, America, Yugoslavia, and Macedonia. My family has two television sets. I can watch the movies we like. I can watch the World Cup.

There is no soccer team in my school in America. That I don't like. I played soccer in my school in Yugoslavia. I miss those friends. We all cried when I left. They gave me a soccer ball with my name on it.

I did not speak any English when I came to America. It was very hard. I did not know what people were saying when they spoke to me. I could only look at them and smile. I feel much better now because my English is better.

I thought our house in America would be very big with many windows and a swimming pool. But our house is small with no swimming pool. Still, I don't want to go back to Yugoslavia to live.

Calling America Home

1. What were two major reasons that Van and Vedrom and their families came to America?

   ✳ _____

   _____

   ✳ _____

   _____

2. Who came from a country with a warm climate? _____

3. What do both Van and Vedron miss about their homelands?

   _____

   _____

   _____

4. Name two problems that both Van and Vedron had in common when they first came to the U.S.

   ✳ _____

   _____

   ✳ _____

   _____

5. Why might people from a particular country or group move to the same area?

   _____

   _____

   _____

Calling America Home

Use the chart below to compare and contrast the experiences of Van and Vedron.

	Van	**Vedron**
Birthplace		
Where Lives in the U.S.		
Reasons for Coming to America		
Reactions When First Arrived		
Reactions Now		
What Misses About Birthplace		

WRITING Interview a classmate, friend, neighbor, or someone in your family who is an immigrant. Find out: Why did the person come to America? What did the person think life would be like here? Write an account of what you find out.

HEART THUMPING WORKOUTS

BY BOB HUGEL

RIDE A BIKE
Biking does a great job of raising your heart rate and also strengthening your leg muscles.

You're walking up the stairs on the way to class. A friend mentions yesterday's science class, and you want to throw in your two cents about all the homework you have to do over the weekend. But by the time you reach the top of the second flight, you're so out of breath, the only thing you're ready to throw in is the towel.

What's going on? The last time you checked, you were young and healthy. How come you're gasping for air?

Chances are, you're out of shape. The National Center for Chronic Disease Prevention and Health Promotion has found that about 14 percent of children and teenagers report no recent physical activity. The Center also found that participation in all types of physical activity declines greatly as age or grade in school increases.

That means that many American young people are missing out on the benefits of aerobic (air-OH-bik) exercise, which, along with promoting long-term health, does things like help control your weight, relieve stress, and make you sleep better.

The good news is that it's not hard to get an aerobic workout. You don't have to buy fancy equipment. "You just have to be active," says Greg Welk, director of childhood and adolescent health at the Cooper Institute for Aerobics Research in Dallas, Texas. "An aerobic exercise is anything that increases your heart

READING TIP

The article talks about a problem that many kids have. As you read,

- identify the problem,
- find out why it is a problem,
- learn what can be done to solve the problem, and
- how the solutions can help kids.

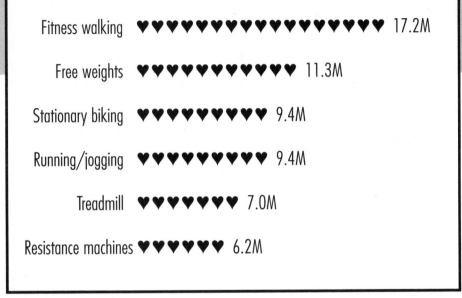

HOW AMERICANS KEEP FIT

About 54 million Americans 6 years and older participate frequently (100 times or more) in fitness activities. This year their top activities, in millions of participants, are:

Fitness walking ♥♥♥♥♥♥♥♥♥♥♥♥♥♥♥♥♥ 17.2M

Free weights ♥♥♥♥♥♥♥♥♥♥♥ 11.3M

Stationary biking ♥♥♥♥♥♥♥♥♥ 9.4M

Running/jogging ♥♥♥♥♥♥♥♥♥ 9.4M

Treadmill ♥♥♥♥♥♥♥ 7.0M

Resistance machines ♥♥♥♥♥♥ 6.2M

PICKUP GAMES
A great way to get an aerobic workout is to play a game like basketball, soccer, or tennis. Find something that's fun. That way you'll be more likely to stick with it.

rate and the amount of oxygen your muscles burn. Brisk walking or yard work are good examples," says Welk. "The activity doesn't have to be extremely rigorous, or hard, as long as you do something that challenges your heart to work harder and get stronger."

What happens if you don't do any type of aerobic activity? Experts say that you're likely to set the tone of your physical health for life. If children and teens are out of shape and overweight, studies show that they're going to continue to get heavier as they get older. Lack of physical activity can also contribute to health problems like heart disease, which can show up later in life.

Fortunately, experts say that just 30 minutes of aerobic exercise a day can help you feel great and live longer. Best of all, it's easy to do. So, get started!

Heart Thumping Workouts

Fill in the circle next to the correct answer.

1. Which activity is <u>not</u> an example of aerobic exercise?

   (A) riding a bike

   (B) playing in a ballgame

   (C) hiking

   (D) riding in a car

2. What is a synonym for the word *rigorous*?

   (A) careful

   (B) difficult

   (C) easy

   (D) lasting a long time

3. According to the article, which statement is true?

   (A) Exercise you do when you're young can affect your health later in life.

   (B) Most children and teenagers get plenty of exercise.

   (C) Five minutes of exercise a day makes your heart stronger.

   (D) Watching a ballgame is good aerobic exercise.

4. The graph shows that the least popular fitness activity is _____ .

   (A) running or jogging

   (B) using resistance machines

   (C) fitness walking

   (D) lifting weights

5. Fitness walking is probably the most popular exercise because _____.

   (A) it doesn't cost anything

   (B) you can do it with friends

   (C) you don't need any special equipment

   (D) all of the above

Heart Thumping Workouts

Fill in the graphic organizer below. First, tell what the problem is. Why is it a problem? Then, list possible solutions that the author recommends. Finally, tell how these solutions will help kids.

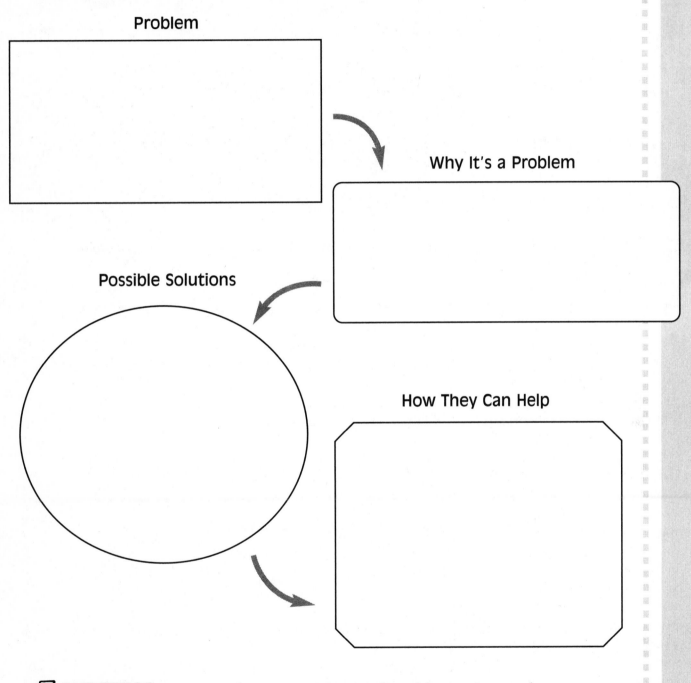

Problem

Why It's a Problem

Possible Solutions

How They Can Help

WRITING Figure out how many minutes of aerobic exercise you do every day. (Physical education class counts!) First, make a list of your daily activities that count as aerobic exercise. Next to each activity, write the number of minutes you spend on it. How do you rate? If you do less than 30 minutes of aerobic exercise a day, write a workout plan for yourself.

From Pampas to Patagonia

The Lands of Southern South America

Paraguay (PAR-uh-gwhy), Uruguay (YOUR-uh-gwhy), southern Chile, and Argentina make up Southern South America. Even though the southern tip of South America is stormy and freezing cold, it is called Tierra del Fuego, or Land of Fire. Spanish explorers gave it this name 500 years ago when they saw Indians there building campfires.

Most of Paraguay is a dry, windy plain called the Gran Chaco. Very few people live there. They live in the eastern part of the country. Uruguay is one of the smallest countries in South America. Most of the country is grassland, which is perfect for raising cattle and sheep.

Top: In Argentina, cowboys called gauchos (GOW-chose) round up cattle on the pampas.

South America

| 0 | 250 | 500 | 750 mi |
| 0 | 250 | 500 | 750 | 1000 km |

FACT FILE
South America

- The continent of South America is shaped like a long triangle. Most of it is south of the equator.
- The climate changes greatly as you travel south. The north and the middle of the continent are hot and rainy. The southern tip is cold and barren, close to the icy continent of Antarctica.

ANIMALS AND PLANTS

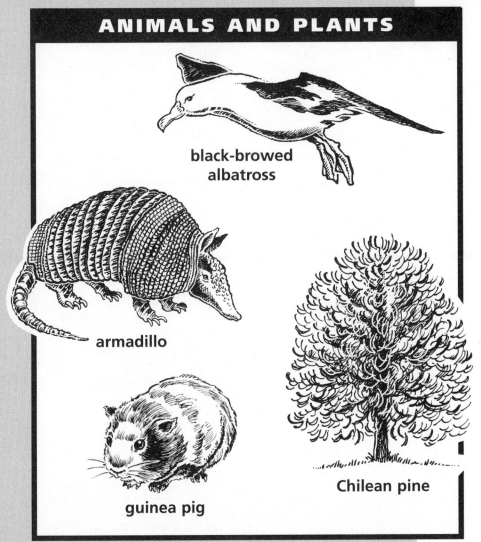

black-browed albatross

armadillo

guinea pig

Chilean pine

Running down the west coast of Southern South America is Chile. Southern Chile is one of the world's wettest and stormiest places.

To the east of Chile lies Argentina. Argentina is the largest country in Southern South America. One out of every three people lives in the capital city of Buenos Aires. The pampas, or grassy plains of central Argentina, are good for raising sheep and cattle. Patagonia (pat-uh-GO-nee-uh) in southern Argentina, is a very cold, windy region. There are no trees, but there is lots of grass for sheep to eat. The town of Ushuaia (ooh-SHY-ah), near Cape Horn, is farther south than any other town in the world. If you sailed east around the world from Ushuaia, you would end up back where you started without ever seeing land!

Top: Cold winds from Antarctica bring snow and ice to Patagonia.

From Pampas to Patagonia

Fill in the circle next to the correct answer.

1. Which country in Southern South America is landlocked, with no outlet to the sea?

   (A) Uruguay

   (B) Chile

   (C) Argentina

   (D) Paraguay

2. The pampas are _____.

   (A) grasslands

   (B) deserts

   (C) mountain ranges

   (D) rain forests

3. It is most likely that Patagonia is a place where _____ .

   (A) many people live

   (B) very few people live

   (C) no one lives

   (D) the population is the same as Buenos Aires

4. Cape Horn is close to _____.

   (A) the equator

   (B) Alaska

   (C) Africa

   (D) Antarctica

5. Underline or highlight the sentences in the article that tell where sheep or cattle are raised. Then write the names of the places here.

   _____

   _____

   _____

From Pampas to Patagonia

FACT SHEET

Create a fact sheet for the countries of Southern South America. Write three or more details for each country.

CHILE

* _____
* _____
* _____
* _____

PARAGUAY

* _____
* _____
* _____
* _____

URUGUAY

* _____
* _____
* _____
* _____

ARGENTINA

* _____
* _____
* _____
* _____

WRITING Write a paragraph for a travel brochure about one of the countries or regions of Southern South America. Tell what the traveler would find there and why the place is interesting to visit. Find out more information if you need it.

Beastly Bugs or Cool Critters?

By Briana Collins

Imagine you've just settled down for an afternoon nap. Suddenly, you feel something creepy crawling up your arm. Its six legs scuttle across your shoulder to tickle your neck. Your hand whips around, ready to whap the pesky insect. BUT WAIT!

Are insects annoying pests or amazing creatures? Insects of all sorts do really cool things. So stop swatting and start reading to get the buzz on bugs!

▼ Good Looker

Without turning your head, can you see what is going on behind you? What about above you? You only have two eyes, both on the front of your face. But a fly has five eyes: three simple eyes called ocelli (OH-sell-eye) on its forehead, and two compound eyes made up of hundreds of smaller lenses. Since its eyes wrap around the sides, top, and bottom of its head, a fly can see in almost all directions. So if you've ever wondered why that pesky fly won't leave you alone, now you know: It only has eyes for you!

This big-eyed horsefly hangs out in pastures where it feeds on the blood of grazing animals.

The thorny dragon grasshopper is found in the rain forests of Malaysia.

▲ Dressed to Kill

The thorny dragon grasshopper looks as though it's dressed for a costume party. But its beady eyes and thorny body actually help the grasshopper scare off predators, or enemies, like birds and bats. The swordlike points on this insect's body act as a caution sign to enemies: "Keep Off!" If a predator ignores the warning, the grasshopper pulls out its next line of defense–its big overbite. Watch out! These teethlike chompers, called mandibles (MAN-dih-bulls), can draw blood!

FACT FILE
What is an insect?

- An insect is an animal.
- An insect has three body parts: a head, thorax, and abdomen.
- An insect has six jointed legs.
- An adult insect usually has wings.
- An insect often has two antennae (an-TEN-ee).

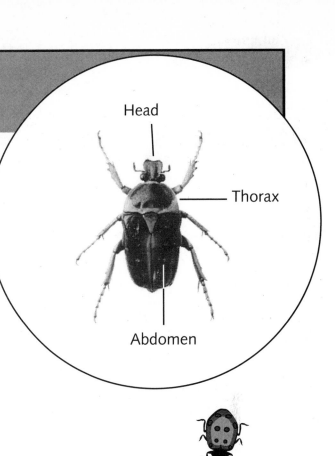

Head

Thorax

Abdomen

What's the Buzz?

- Grasshoppers have 900 separate muscles, and caterpillars have as many as 4,000. Compare that to humans, who only have 792 distinct muscles!
- For every person on the planet, there are about 20,000 mosquitoes.

Stink Bomber

This bombardier (bom-buh-DEER) beetle, native to New Mexico, looks harmless. But invade this guy's turf and ZAP! A shot of smelly, hot liquid explodes in your face. When attacked, the beetle needs time to unfold its covered wings. So it takes aim at its enemy and shoots out a liquid that it mixes in a sac in its abdomen. The mixture of boiling-hot chemicals is strong enough to stop an insect predator in its path. This buys time for the beetle to open its wings and clears the runway for takeoff.

When a bombardier beetle sprays a human, the person feels a burning sensation.

Beastly Bugs or Cool Critters?

Fill in the circle next to the correct answer.

1. The insect population is _____ the human population.

   (A) smaller than

   (B) the same as

   (C) growing faster than

   (D) larger than

2. A predator is _____ .

   (A) an insect

   (B) a scientist who studies insects

   (C) an animal's enemy

   (D) a male grasshopper

3. The thorny dragon grasshopper scares off enemies _____.

   (A) because of its strong smell

   (B) because of the sharp points on its body

   (C) by spraying a liquid

   (D) by making a loud noise

Write your answers to the following questions.

4. Compare the spider with the insect at the top of page 59.

   How many body parts does the spider have? _____

   How many legs does the spider have? _____

   Does the spider have wings? _____

   Does the spider have antennae? _____

   Based on your answers, is a spider a type of insect? _____

Beastly Bugs or Cool Critters?

Record each insect's defense against predators.

Insect	Defense Against Predators
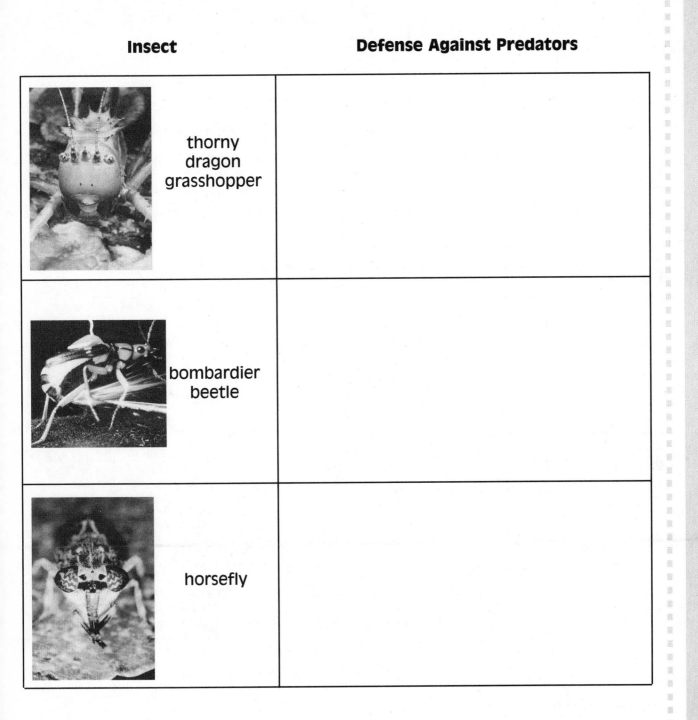 thorny dragon grasshopper	
bombardier beetle	
horsefly	

 WRITING Are insects amazing creatures or annoying pests? What's your opinion? Give your reasons for thinking as you do.

SEQUOYAH AND THE CHEROKEE

NATIVE PEOPLES OF THE SOUTHEAST

Long ago the continent of North America was home to many Native American peoples. Their cultures varied from one region to another. Most Native Americans who lived in the Southeast farmed and hunted for food. They built wooden houses around a central community house.

The Cherokee

Many groups of people lived in the Southeast. The Cherokee were among them. They called themselves Aniyunwiya (ahn-uh-YEWN-wee-yah), or "first people." By 1770 they numbered about 12,000. The Cherokee originally lived in the area of the Great Lakes. The moved—no one knows exactly when—to an area that is now part of Georgia, Tennessee, North Carolina, and Alabama. One famous Cherokee was Sequoyah, who was also known as George Guess. He accomplished a great thing for his people. He also lived through the difficult changes his people faced.

This map shows some of the Southeast's major Native American groups.

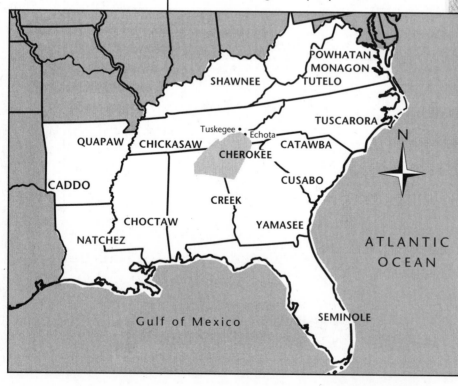

"The children must learn to write and read our language," said Sequoyah (sih-KWOY-uh) in 1809. He wanted his people, the Cherokee, to record their past in writing so they would not forget it. He set himself an incredible task: inventing a way to write the Cherokee language.

SEQUOYAH'S ALPHABET

Sequoyah was born around 1760 in the Cherokee village of Tuskegee (tus-KEE-gee). This village was located in what is today Tennessee. It was one of more than 40 Cherokee communities in the region.

As a boy Sequoyah was interested in the stories his grandfather and other storytellers told. He was fascinated by the adventures they described.

As he grew older, Sequoyah worried that people might not remember Cherokee history and culture. After talking with Sequoyah, a writer named Jeremiah Evarts said:

> *Sequoyah had observed white people writing things on paper, and he had seen books; and he knew that what was written down remained and was not forgotten.*

A Cherokee Alphabet

In 1809 Sequoyah started to work on a written language. He thought hard about the words of his language. He realized each word was made up of smaller sounds, or syllables. He decided to give a symbol to each of these syllables. This system is called a syllabary (SIH-luh-beh-ree). Sequoyah borrowed some of his symbols from the English and Greek alphabets. Yet the sounds they represent are not the same. When he was finished, he had 86 symbols.

Sequoyah's Cherokee syllabary was completed in 1821. Some Cherokee were suspicious of his written language at first. Soon, though, they found how useful it was. By February 1828, the first issue of the *Cherokee Phoenix* rolled off a printing press in Georgia. It was the first newspaper ever printed by Native Americans in one of their own languages.

CHEROKEE ALPHABET.

CHARACTERS AS ARRANGED BY THE INVENTOR.

R D W h G S W P A ϟ Y Ꮣ Ꮮ P Ꮞ M C Ꮿ Ꭴ
Ꮙ W B Ꭰ Ꭰ Ꮧ Ꮵ Ꭶ Ꮄ Ꭺ Ꭻ Ᏼ Ꮯ Ꮲ Ꮐ Ꮓ Ꮈ Ꮀ Ꮶ I Z Ꮩ
Ꮳ Ꭼ Ꮂ Ꮝ Ꭺ Ꭾ Ꮐ Ꮞ Ꮦ Ꮞ Ꮚ Ꭶ Ꮧ Ꮞ J K Ꮒ Ꮹ Ꮄ
Ꮳ Ꮖ Ꭲ Ꭸ Ꮝ Ꮲ Ꮆ Ꮧ Ꮝ Ꮿ Ꮲ Ꮴ Ꮶ Ꮅ Ꮌ Ꮮ
L Ꮤ Ꮔ Ꮠ Ꮅ Ꮞ

CHARACTERS SYSTEMATICALLY ARRANGED WITH THE SOUNDS.

D a	R e	T i	Ꮼ o	Ꮕ u	i v
Ꭶ ga Ꭺ ka	Ꮄ ge	y gi	A go	J gu	E gv
Ꭿ ha	Ꭾ he	Ꭺ hi	Ꭽ ho	Ꭲ hu	Ꭴ hv
W la	Ꮄ le	Ꮅ li	Ꮆ lo	Ꮇ lu	Ꮈ lv
Ꮉ ma	Ꮊ me	H mi	Ꮋ mo	Ꮌ mu	
Ꮎ na Ꮏ hna Ꮐ nah Ꮑ ne	Ꮒ ni	Z no	Ꮔ nu	Ꮕ nv	
Ꮖ qua	Ꮗ que	Ꮘ qui	Ꮙ quo	Ꮚ quu	Ꮛ quv
Ꮝ Ꮜ sa	4 se	Ꮢ si	Ꮠ so	Ꮡ su	R sv
Ꮤ da W ta	Ꮞ de Ꮢ te	Ꮧ di Ꮣ tih A do	s du	Ꮩ dv	
Ꮫ dla Ꮭ tla	L tle	Ꮏ tli	Ꮬ tlo	Ꮰ tlu	P tlv
Ꮳ tsa	Ꮴ tse	Ꮪ tsi	K tso	J tsu	Ꮶ tsv
Ꮹ wa	Ꮺ we	Ꮻ wi	Ꮼ wo	Ꮽ wu	Ꮾ wv
Ꭷ ya	Ꮿ ye	Ꮵ yi	Ꮸ yo	Ꮕ yu	B yv

SOUNDS REPRESENTED BY VOWELS.

a as *a* in *father*, or short as *a* in *rival*,
e as *a* in *hate*, or short as *e* in *met*,
i as *i* in *pique*, or short as *i* in *pit*,
o as *aw* in *law*, or short as *o* in *not*,
u as *oo* in *fool*, or short as *u* in *pull*,
v as *u* in *but* nasalized.

CONSONANT SOUNDS.

g nearly as in English, but approaching to k. d nearly as in English, but approaching to t. h, k, l, m, n, q, s, t, w, y, as in English.

Syllables beginning with g, except Ꮝ, have sometimes the power of k; Ꭺ, Ꮝ, Ꮿ, are sometimes sounded to, tu, tv; and syllables written with tl, except Ꮭ, sometimes vary to dl.

THE TRAIL OF TEARS

During the early 1800s white settlers began moving onto Native American lands. The United States government decided that the Cherokee and other Native Americans had to leave to make room for these settlers.

A Terrible Journey

Most Cherokee wished to remain near their homelands in the Southeast. Some fled into the Great Smoky Mountains. In 1838, though, the United States Army forced most of them to move hundreds of miles west to Arkansas and Oklahoma.

About 15,000 Cherokee had to leave the Southeast. Disease and cold killed 4,000 people on the journey. Those who survived remembered it as the **Trail of Tears**. Yet they worked hard to build a life in their new land. Soon there was a new Cherokee capital at Tahlequah (TAH-lah-kwah), Oklahoma. Sequoyah taught many people his syllabary.

THE CHEROKEE TODAY

A few years after the Trail of Tears, nearly all of the Cherokee could read and write their language. Today over 95,000 Cherokee live in Oklahoma. In North Carolina over 10,000 Cherokee live on their ancestors' lands. Though they all speak English, many like to use the Cherokee writing.

Robert Lindneux painted this picture of the Trail of Tears in 1942. Many Cherokee walked for hundreds of miles. The men in tall hats are the United States soldiers.

Sequoyah and the Cherokee

Fill in the circle next to the correct answer.

1. Cherokee lands once extended into _____ present-day states.

    (A) two

    (B) three

    (C) four

    (D) five

2. Today many Cherokee live in _____ .

    (A) Oklahoma and North Carolina

    (B) Alabama and Georgia

    (C) Florida

    (D) Tennessee

3. What kind of language did the Cherokee have before the syllabary?

    (A) a spoken language only

    (B) none

    (C) sign language

    (D) both a spoken and written language

4. What caused Sequoyah to create a syllabary?

    (A) He wanted to publish a newspaper.

    (B) He was afraid Cherokee history would be forgotten.

    (C) He liked listening to stories.

    (D) The U.S. government required that he do so.

5. What were the effects of having a syllabary? List some of the ways Sequoyah's alphabet helped the Cherokee.

    _____

    _____

    _____

Sequoyah and the Cherokee

Before you read the article, preview the text. Then fill out the prereading organizer below and predict what you think the article will be about. After you read, look at your predictions to see if they were correct.

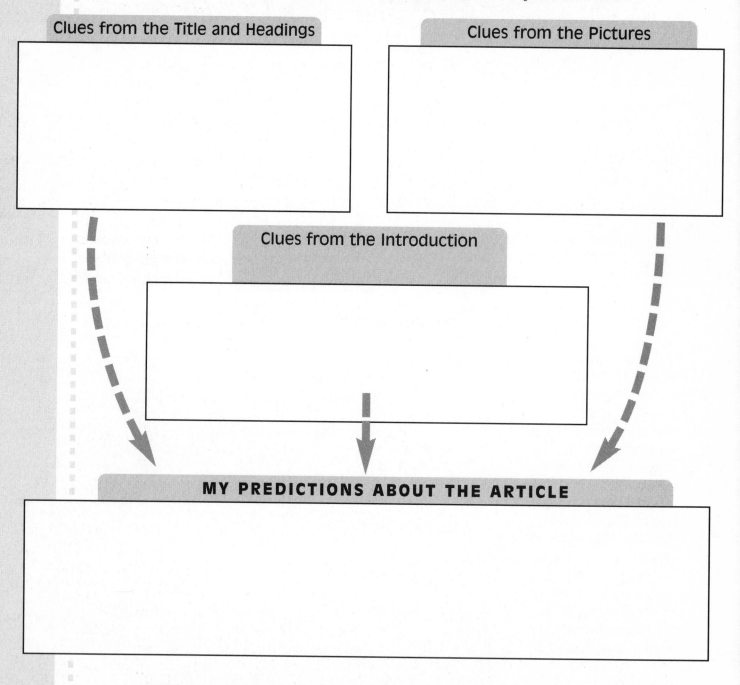

Clues from the Title and Headings

Clues from the Pictures

Clues from the Introduction

MY PREDICTIONS ABOUT THE ARTICLE

AFTER READING Were your predictions correct? ❑ YES ❑ NO

WRITING Imagine that you are a newspaper reporter in 1821. Write an interview with Sequoyah about his new Cherokee syllabary.

Nancy Ward: Revolutionary War Leader

By Diane Silcox-Jarrett

Twenty years before the American Revolutionary War, during a battle with the Creek Indians, Nancy Ward saw her husband die.

He was the Cherokee chief and a great warrior. His death caused confusion and uncertainty among the Cherokees. Nancy had rushed into the fight and picked up his bow and arrow. She then led her tribe to victory.

Nancy had earned the name Agi-ga-u-e or "Beloved Woman" of the Cherokee tribe because of this deed. This name was a title of recognition and importance. With it she became the head of the Women's Council and also sat as a member of the Council of Chiefs. These were not mere honorary positions. In Cherokee society women owned the land and the wealth. It was passed from mother to daughter. When a

Cherokee Life

The Cherokees lived in permanent towns. Each town has 30–60 log cabins built around a large central meeting hall. Women grew crops and provided the majority of the food, while men hunted. In the central meeting hall special occasions like weddings and funerals were held. All the important decisions were made there too. With priests, chiefs, elders and beloved women leading the discussions, the Cherokees' goal for tribal harmony rested on everyone agreeing to important decisions. If one person disagreed with the whole town, he or she might be banned and sent away. ❧

couple married, the husband moved into the woman's house, and if they divorced, the man had to move out. Women had an equal say with men on war councils and treaty negotiations. The Women's Council could override decisions that men made. Leading the Women's Council was a great honor and a highly responsible position.

Nancy Ward's given name was Nanye-hi, but the white settlers called her Nancy. She befriended the Patriot settlers who came to her valley along the Tennessee River. Nancy always hoped her people would live in peace with them. When the British offered to pay Cherokee warriors to attack Patriot settlers, she ran to tell her friend, John Sevier. Arriving at his house, she was out of breath.

"What is the matter, Nancy?" John asked as he opened the door and saw her worried face.

"There's going to be an attack," she said, breathing hard. "It is going to be soon. I overheard some of the men talking." John helped Nancy into his house and offered her a drink of water.

"What type of attack are they planning?" he asked.

"Some Cherokees will attack those of you who are not loyal to the British king. The British are offering rewards to warriors who will fight," she answered.

FACT FILE
Cherokee

- They are currently the largest Native American tribe in the U.S.
- They originally lived in the southern Appalachian region.
- In 1838–1839 the Cherokee were forced to leave their homes and move to a reservation in Oklahoma. Because many died, this is known as the Trail of Tears
- In 1821, a Cherokee named Sequoyah created a writing system for spoken Cherokee.

Then she drank deeply, "I really must get back," she said standing up. "I don't want anyone to know that I have come here to talk to you."

"Thank you, Nancy," John said as he walked her to the door. "I'll tell everyone and we'll be prepared." The Patriot settlers turned back the Cherokee attack because of Nancy's warning. They punished the warriors who fought for the British by destroying Cherokee settlements, but those of Nancy's Chota clan were left untouched.

In 1780, Nancy once again warned the Patriot settlers about another attack. When the settlers organized themselves for the battle, Nancy went to them and tried to find some way the two sides could compromise. When she failed, the Patriot settlers destroyed more Cherokee towns. When the two sides met after the battle Nancy once again urged a compromise between the Cherokee and Patriot settlers. She spoke eloquently for a "chain of friendship" between the two groups. Nancy was a main voice when the Treaty of Hopewell was signed in 1785.

Nancy's hope that the native people and the settlers would learn to live with each other in peace never left her. She died in 1822 and was buried in the Tennessee hills she loved.

Nancy Ward: Revolutionary War Leader

Fill in the circle next to the correct answer.

1. Which statement does <u>not</u> describe Nancy Ward.

   (A) She was a brave fighter for her people.

   (B) She prevented the destruction of her clan's homes.

   (C) She helped govern her people.

   (D) She lived with the settlers to save her people.

2. Which happened first?

   (A) The Revolutionary War began.

   (B) The Treaty of Hopewell was signed.

   (C) Nancy Ward warned the Patriot settlers about a British attack.

   (D) Nancy Ward's husband died.

3. Nancy *befriended* the Patriot settlers. That means she _____

   (A) became their enemy.

   (B) helped them grow crops.

   (C) lived in peace with them.

   (D) was very unfriendly toward them.

4. Nancy Ward's husband died _____

   (A) during the Revolutionary War.

   (B) due to an illness.

   (C) during a battle with a neighboring tribe.

   (D) while fighting against the Patriots.

5. List three facts you learned about how Cherokee women lived during the late 1700s.

   _____

   _____

   _____

Nancy Ward: Revolutionary War Leader

Create a time line showing the important events in Nancy Ward's life.

mid-1700s _____

_____

_____

_____

_____

1780 _____

_____

_____

1785 _____

_____

_____

1822 _____

_____

_____

_____

 WRITING Research another famous Revolutionary War–era woman. These include Abigail Adams, Sybil Ludington, Rebecca Motte, Molly Hays McCauley, Esther Reed, Betsy Ross, Deborah Sampson, Phillis Wheatley, Patience Wright, Elizabeth Zane, and Prudence Wright.

CHANGE OF HEART

When U.S. hockey team forward Shelley Looney chases a puck across the rink, her heart is pounding. But she's not nervous. Looney's fast heartbeat is helping her keep up with the **zooming** puck.

Fact
The human heart is the size of a fist. It beats 80 times per minute.

Survival Tip
Stay active to keep your heart healthy.

When Looney skates hard, her muscles need energy. With each beat, her heart pushes blood loaded with oxygen and nutrients through a network of arteries and capillaries.

The blood returns through veins to the heart. Looney's circulatory system **assists** her in other ways, too. During exercise, her blood vessels dilate, or grow wider, so more blood can flow through them.

Humans aren't the only animals who can have a change of heart. The circulatory systems of whales, hummingbirds, and hibernating **creatures** such as groundhogs adjust so they can survive special situations.

SLOW BEAT

When a whale plunges hundreds of meters beneath the ocean's surface to search for food, its nervous system signals, "Slow down. Save oxygen." Its heart slows down and practically stops. The blood vessels in its fins, tail, and stomach pinch shut. Only blood vessels to the heart and brain stay open to ensure an oxygen supply for the brain, the animal's control center.

This is called dive response. It helps the whale survive underwater without a breath for 20 minutes or more.

Fact
A humpback whale's heart is the size of a large oil drum. It beats 10–20 times per minute.

Survival Tip
It can slow its heart rate during long, deep dives for food.

All mammals have a dive response—including humans. Your heart rate drops when you jump into water. It also slows down when you're sleeping or resting.

SURVIVAL SPEED

On dry land, hibernating animals can be **dormant**, or inactive, for days at a time. They can survive without food and water with a body temperature close to freezing. Their heart is one reason why. During hibernation, for example, the groundhog's heart slows from a normal rate of 120 beats per minute to an incredibly slow six beats per minute. Just as the dive response helps a whale go deep, hibernation allows the groundhog to make it through a time when there is little or no food available.

Even tiny hummingbirds can save energy by slowing their heart **rate**. In flight, their hearts beat more than 1,200 times per minute. But at night, they let their bodies cool so they don't need much energy. In a sluggish state called torpor, a hummingbird's heart slows to 50 beats a minute.

Of course, there's more to surviving the cold than having a slow heart rate. Hibernating animals have

Fact
A hummingbird's heart is the size of a pea. It beats 1,200 beats per minute while flying.

Survival Tip
It can slow its heart rate to save energy.

adapted in other ways as well. Special chemicals in each cell of a hibernating animal's body protect the animal's tissues and organs from freezing. And while blood may drain from the paws, fins, and tails of these animals, there is one place where blood flow remains close to normal—the animal's brain.

Fact
A groundhog's heart is the size of a plum. It beats 120 times per minute.

Survival Tip
It can slow its heart rate to 6 beats per minute during hibernation.

WORD WISE

assist To help.

creature A living being, such as a human or animal.

dormant Not active.

rate Speed or pace.

zooming Moving quickly, rising rapidly and suddenly.

To see an animation of blood flowing through a human heart, visit: www.pbs.org/wgbh/nova/heart/heartmap.html.

Change of Heart

Fill in the circle next to the correct answer.

1. What is the main idea of this article?

   (A) Your heart is part of your circulatory system.

   (B) The circulatory systems of animals and humans change to help them survive.

   (C) Whales, hummingbirds, groundhogs, and humans have hearts.

   (D) Animals and humans have many systems working in their bodies, including the circulatory and nervous systems.

2. A groundhog's heart slows down when it hibernates in order to _____.

   (A) stay warm

   (B) sleep longer

   (C) save energy

   (D) freeze it

3. During exercise, your heart rate _____.

   (A) increases and blood vessels contract

   (B) decreases and blood vessels contract

   (C) increases and blood vessels enlarge

   (D) stays the same

4. Which animal's heart beats the fastest?

   (A) whale

   (B) aardvark

   (C) groundhog

   (D) hummingbird

5. Draw a circle around each animal named in the article. Underline the sentences that state how its heart rate changes to help it survive.

Change of Heart

Compare the hearts and heart rates of the animals listed in each diagram.

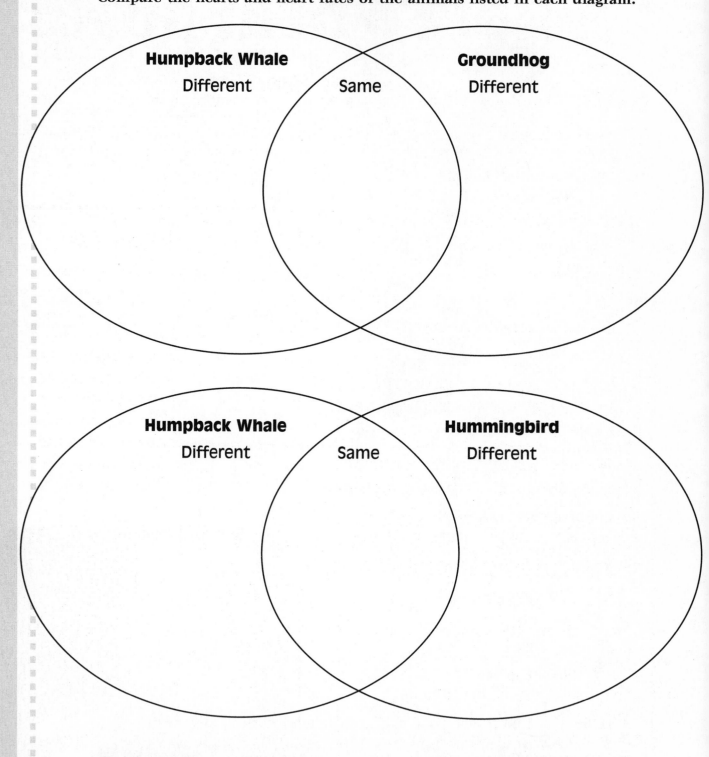

WRITING Select another animal. Find out the size of its heart, how fast it beats, and how it adapts to special situations. Create an Animal Fact Card for this animal, using the fact circles in the article as a model.

Nonfiction Passages With Graphic Organizers for Independent Practice

Nature's Neat Noses

By Emily Costello

Animals of all sorts have noses. They use them to smell, snoop, snort, sneeze, and more. An elephant can suck water with its nose and snort it out for a slightly slimy shower.

Loud Honker

Proboscis (pro-BAH-sis) is another word for nose. Can you guess how this **proboscis monkey** got its name? The monkey's nose never stops growing. It even gets in the way of eating! The long nose helps the monkey warn others of danger. The male makes a loud honk with its nose. The long nose acts as a loudspeaker, amplifying the sound.

Long-Distance Smell

Life is short for the **North American moon moth**. The male moth lives only seven days, so he can't waste time finding a mate. Luckily, his nose—two super-sensitive feathery **antennae** (a pair of sensory organs on his head)—helps him sniff out female moths of the same species up to seven miles away. Scientists think the moon moth may have the most sensitive nose in the animal kingdom!

Termite Sniffer

Anteaters live in Central and South America. This toothless **mammal** (a warm-blooded animal that has hair and feeds its young with milk) has a super-long nose that sniffs out termite and ant nests hidden in grass. The anteater digs up the nests with its long, sharp claws. While the dirt flies, the anteater closes up its nostrils. Then, out darts the anteater's 24-inch (61 centimeter) long tongue to suck up tasty termites.

Did You Know?

- A mosquito smells with its mouth, not its nose.
- An earthworm smells with its skin.

Noisy Nose

Echoes help **Honduran white bats** find food and fly safely at night. This Central American bat uses its nose to snort out a series of high-pitched noises. The nose's leaf shape gives the bat better aim and volume control. Then the bat uses its ears to listen for noises bouncing back, a process that is called **echolocation**. This way, the bat can "see" bugs and steer a clear path through the dark sky.

Nature's Neat Noses

Fill in the circle next to the correct answer.

1. Which animal does <u>not</u> smell with a nose?

   (A) human being

   (B) proboscis monkey

   (C) anteater

   (D) mosquito

2. Which statement supports the idea that animal noses have more than one function?

   (A) Anteaters are toothless mammals that eat ants and termites.

   (B) An elephant can suck water with its nose and snort it out for a shower.

   (C) Animal noses can be different sizes and shapes.

   (D) A mosquito smells with its mouth.

3. Which sentence uses the word *proboscis* correctly?

   (A) My proboscis is all stuffed up, and I can't smell a thing.

   (B) The eye doctor checked my proboscis and prescribed new glasses.

   (C) I've outgrown my proboscis and need to buy a new one.

   (D) I left my proboscis on the bus by mistake.

4. The _____ smells with its skin.

   (A) anteater

   (B) mosquito

   (C) earthworm

   (D) moon moth

5. Which animal nose do you think is the "neatest"? Why?

   _____

   _____

   _____

Nature's Neat Noses

The graphic organizer below is a Feature Analysis Grid. Column 1 tells which animal's nose you are to analyze. The other columns list various features of different animal noses.

STEP 1: Read each animal name. Then read each feature.

STEP 2: If the animal has the feature, write a **+** sign in that column.

STEP 3: If the animal does not have the feature, write a **−** sign in that column.

STEP 4: If the article does not give information about the feature, write **?** in the column.

Then use the finished grid to compare and contrast animal noses.

FEATURE

ANIMAL	nose is on face	nose is not on face	nose makes noises	nose used only to smell with	nose is very long
moon moth					
proboscis monkey					
anteater					
Honduran white bat					

WRITING Do some research about the elephant's nose. What can it do, in addition to smell? What unusual features does it have? Create a fact file that could be added to "Nature's Neat Noses" telling the information that you learn.

Twister!

December 6, 2003

By Steph Smith

Tornadoes tear through the eastern half
of the United States each year.
What causes these deadly wind storms?

READING TIP

The article you are about
to read explains the causes and
effects of tornadoes. As you
read,

- identify the causes, or what
  happens
- find out why these things
  happen, or the effects
- look for key words such
  as *because, then,* and
  as a result

Nine-year-old Justin Henry of Mossy Grove, Tennessee, met a force so powerful that it lifted him into midair. It sucked the shoes off his feet. Justin's mom had to grab his ankles to stop the "monster" from taking him, too.

Justin had just come face-to-face with a tornado, one of nature's most violent and destructive storms. Tornadoes are spinning columns of air that stretch from a storm cloud down to the ground. They can reach speeds of more than 250 mph.

The Henry family's home was destroyed, but the family survived. They are just one of many families across the South and Midwest who must rebuild their lives. More than 70 tornadoes touched down in the eastern half of the U.S. last month. The storms stretched from Louisiana to Pennsylvania. In some cases, entire communities were destroyed. The tornadoes demolished houses, pulled trees from the ground, snapped telephone poles, and threw cars and trucks several yards through the air. Dozens of people were killed. Ohio, Tennessee, and Alabama were the hardest hit.

"Yesterday, we had a nice brick house and four vehicles," said Justin's mom, Susan. "Today, we don't own a toothbrush."

Surprising But Explainable

The deadly weather caught many Americans off guard. Tornadoes in the U.S. occur mostly in spring and summer, and often touch down in "tornado alley," an area between central Texas and Nebraska.

Generally, tornadoes develop one at a time. Last month's weather system produced a swarm of them. Weather experts say it was one of the worst November tornado outbreaks ever.

Why did it happen? Conditions were ripe for a tornado outbreak. Warm air headed north from the Gulf of Mexico pushed under a massive layer of cold air headed east that stretched from Texas to New York. The collision of cold air and warm air often causes violent thunderstorms called supercells. Supercells produce tornadoes. This

HOW TORNADOES FORM

Scientists aren't exactly sure how tornadoes develop. But they have some pretty good ideas:

❶ Tornadoes are born of violent thunderstorms called supercells. Supercells often begin to take shape when warm, moist air pushes through cool, dry air.

❷ Different forces work together to make the rising, warm air begin to spiral.

❸ The spiral intensifies as rain from the thunderstorm drives cold air down the spiral.

❹ Cold air at lower heights can sometimes form a cloud at the base of this massive storm. The vast intensity of the spiraling air can then cause what's known as a tornado to extend from this cloud to the ground.

type of weather condition is common in the U.S., making tornadoes, in general, commonplace. In fact, the U.S. is the tornado capital of the world. About 1,000 tornadoes touch down each year. They have struck every U.S. state, including Alaska and Hawaii.

Surviving Deadly Weather

Quick thinking helped many people survive the recent twisters. A tornado in Van Wert, Ohio, ripped the top off a movie theater just minutes after a showing of Santa Claus 2. No one was hurt because the theater manager had been warned of the tornado by a tornado alert system. He told the moviegoers to take shelter in sturdier parts of the building. They all survived. See the tips that follow on what to do if a tornado touches down near you.

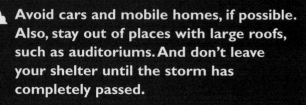

IF A TWISTER HITS . . .

Seek Shelter: A basement is best. Rooms without windows, such as closets, are also good shelters.

Protect Yourself: Get under a piece of furniture and/or wrap yourself in a blanket to protect yourself from falling debris. Cover your head and neck with your arms.

Avoid cars and mobile homes, if possible. Also, stay out of places with large roofs, such as auditoriums. And don't leave your shelter until the storm has completely passed.

Twister!

Fill in the circle next to the correct answer.

1. The area between central Texas and Nebraska is called "tornado alley" because _____ .

   Ⓐ tornadoes only happen there

   Ⓑ the worst tornadoes have hit there

   Ⓒ tornadoes are very common there

   Ⓓ people are ready for tornadoes there

2. Which of the following should you <u>not</u> do during a tornado warning?

   Ⓐ go to the basement

   Ⓑ hide in your car

   Ⓒ get under a table

   Ⓓ go to a room with no windows

3. Tornadoes occur _____.

   Ⓐ when air begins moving and spinning quickly

   Ⓑ when thunderstorms occur over several days

   Ⓒ when warm, wet air pushes through cool, dry air

   Ⓓ when rainstorms get very heavy

4. Which of the following is true?

   Ⓐ Tornadoes develop out of powerful thunderstorms called supercells.

   Ⓑ Tornadoes can destroy houses, trees, and large buildings.

   Ⓒ Tornadoes have hit every state in the U.S.

   Ⓓ All of the above.

5. Ⓒircle the section of the article that details how you can keep yourself safer during a tornado.

Twister!

Complete the chart below with information from the article.

Effect

TORNADOES

⬇

Causes

_____

_____

_____

_____

_____

Where They Occur	**How People Protect Themselves**
_____	_____
_____	_____
_____	_____
_____	_____
_____	_____

WRITING Research the causes and effects of another natural occurrence, such as a hurricane, earthquake, volcanic eruption, or tsunami.

Women's RIGHTS

FACT FILE
Roman Numerals

The article you are about to read contains Roman numerals. Use the key below to help you.

I = 1	VI = 6
II = 2	VII = 7
III = 3	VIII = 8
IV = 4	IX = 9
V = 5	X = 10

Women all over the world have had to struggle to gain equal rights—including women in the United States. It was not that long ago that American women could not vote, hold down certain jobs, or even play certain sports. Many American women have worked hard to change that. While there is still work to be done, many roadblocks to American women's liberties are now history. Below is a time line of how far women in the U.S. have come in the last 80 or so years.

1920

The 19th Amendment to the U.S. Constitution is ratified, giving American women the right to vote.

1942

Women leave their jobs in the home to help out during World War II (1941–1945). About 350,000 women join the armed forces, many serving as nurses. Several million work in factories making products used during the war. After the war, most of the women's jobs are given back to men returning from the fighting. Women are expected to return home and raise families. Those who keep working are paid less than men.

1964

Congress passes the Civil Rights act, outlawing many types of discrimination, including discrimination against women in the workplace. A women's rights movement emerges in the 1960s and 1970s that focuses on women's limited professional choices and unequal wages. Women protest to get equal access to jobs traditionally held by men, and to be granted equal pay and treatment when performing those jobs.

1972

Congress passes a law known as Title IX (nine). The law states that schools receiving federal funds can't discriminate based on gender. Girls' sports programs now must receive the same funds as boys' sports programs. Before that, boys' sports programs were getting more money than girls'.

1978

For the first time in history, more women than men enter colleges in the U.S.

1981

Sandra Day O'Connor becomes the first woman to be appointed to the U.S. Supreme Court. (Today, she and Ruth Bader Ginsburg, appointed in 1993, are the only two women on the nine-member Supreme Court.) There is one woman in the 100-member U.S. Senate in the early 1980s. By 1987, two women are in the Senate.

1990s

Women make up almost half of the U.S. workforce by the mid-1990s.

2002

Thirteen women serve in the U.S. Senate, and 62 women serve in the 435-member U.S. House of Representatives, the most women ever in Congress.

It's About Time! Women's Rights

Fill in the circle next to the correct answer.

1. When did women first get the right to vote?

   (A) 1776

   (B) 1865

   (C) 1920

   (D) 2003

2. How did Title IX help women?

   (A) Women could now serve on the Supreme Court.

   (B) Women could now vote.

   (C) Women could no longer get less pay for the same job.

   (D) Women's sports programs had to get the same money as men's.

3. Which happened first?

   (A) A woman became a U.S. Supreme Court Justice.

   (B) Women went to work to help during World War II.

   (C) Women were allowed to vote.

   (D) More women than men entered U.S. colleges.

4. Which statement is <u>not</u> true?

   (A) At one time women could not vote for President of the United States.

   (B) At one time, women were paid less than men for doing the same job.

   (C) At one time, there were more women than men in the U.S. Congress.

   (D) At one time, there were more men than women in U.S. colleges.

5. <u>Underline</u> the sentences that tell about "firsts" for women, such as the first time they could vote.

It's About Time! Women's Rights

Complete the time line below by summarizing the information in the article. Use one or two sentences to tell about the important event that happened in each year.

1920 _____

_____

_____

1942 _____

_____

_____

1964 _____

_____

_____

1972 _____

_____

_____

1981 _____

_____

_____

2002 _____

_____

_____

WRITING Create a time line showing other historical events during the 1900s. Include facts from the article as well as other facts you read in an encyclopedia.

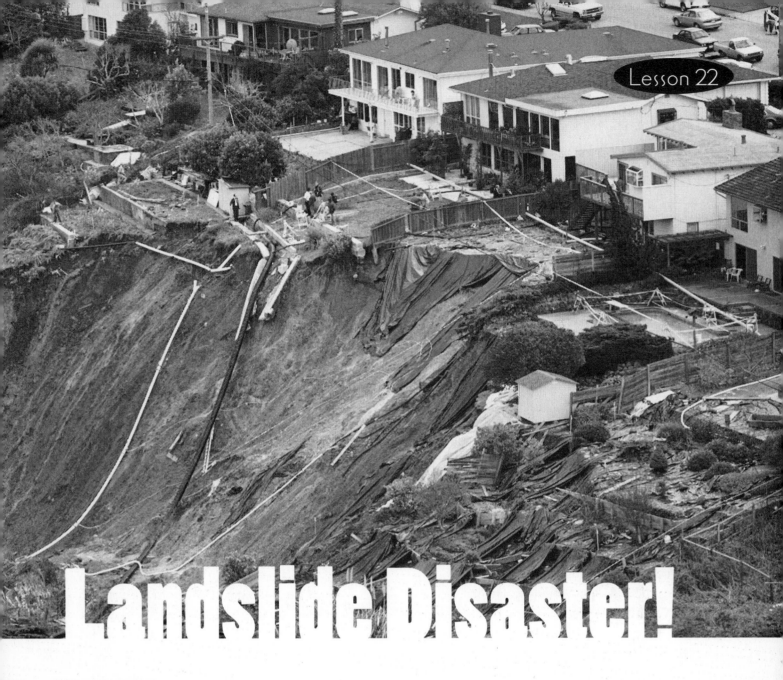

Landslide Disaster!

By Bob Woods

It's raining hard, and Jeanne LePage is out in the front yard of her parents' house in La Honda, California, looking at the lawn. The ground is wrinkled into ridges, instead of lying flat. "It looks like an accordion," Jeanne thinks.

She's worried. Days of rain have soaked the ground. Dark cracks run across the bare hillside behind the LePage's house. The wet soil is pulling away from the hard rock underneath.

Once inside, Jeanne is shocked. The kitchen floor is now tilted, like a fun house! But this is not fun. Jeanne, a student in college, knows that the uneven floor, the cracks in the hillside, and the popping noises neighbors have heard inside their houses are signs that the land under the entire hillside is on the move. Jeanne's family must leave immediately, before the soil breaks from the hill in a landslide.

Landslides are a problem all over the world. In the United States, more than $51 billion a year is spent cleaning up rocks and soil that creeps, slides, and falls. Landslides and rockslides are also dangerous: Between 25 and 50 people in the U.S. lose their lives each year when soil makes a surprising move. The LePages left their house in 1998, days before it and seven others were wrecked by the weight of moving mud. But not all landslides start with the drip-drop of rain.

Some start with a bang!

One of the biggest landslides of the 20th century happened in 1980, just minutes before one of the century's biggest volcanic eruptions—on Mount St. Helens in Washington state. Tons of rock on the side of the mountain suddenly gave way, sliding off a bulge of melted rock, or magma, that had been swelling under it. The landslide traveled faster than a freight train. The slide ended up covering the North Fork Toutle River—in some places as deep as a 60-story building! Minutes later, the top of Mount St. Helens blew off. Hot gases melted snow, causing a flood of water and a giant mudslide.

But it isn't just the heat and power of an eruption that can cause a landslide. Ash from a volcano can pile up in thick layers around the mountain. This is what happened when Mount Pinatubo erupted in the Philippines. For years after this eruption, heavy rains soaked the layers of ash on the volcano's slopes, making it heavy and slippery. The result: Huge, miles-wide mudslides.

Some with a rumble.

What else can move earth? An earthquake. When Earth's crust, or top layer, shifts, an earthquake occurs. Sections of the ground may move centimeters or even meters! The earth can ripple like a wave. All of this movement can literally shake off layers of soil, causing rockslides and landslides on hillsides. After the 1994 Northridge earthquake in California, experts estimated that there were thousands of landslides —some small, others covering roads and houses, taking months to clean up.

One of the worst landslides in recent history occurred in January 2001, in El Salvador in Central America. A strong earthquake shook loose an entire hillside, which tumbled down on top of houses and schools. More than 1,000 people were missing after the slide.

Slide stoppers

Experts can usually predict where land will slide. Usually, if a steep cliff face has fallen before, it will fall again.

Wind, rain, and flowing water can erode, or gradually wear away a hillside, making it steeper. The steeper the hill, the easier it is for rocks and soil to fall down it. Certain types of soil can slide more easily than others: Loose, rocky dirt is an easier slider; soil with lots of clay in it becomes very slippery when wet.

FACT FILE
Ring of Fire

- a zone along the edge of the Pacific Ocean that has many volcanoes and earthquakes
- includes New Zealand, Philippines, Japan, Alaska, Oregon, California, Mexico, and the Andes Mountains of South America
- approximately 350 volcanoes are in the zone

In some cases, trees and grasses can help prevent landslides. Plant roots hold on to soil so there is less erosion. Changing a hillside by removing trees can create a landslide risk: Trees had been recently cut from the hillside in El Salvador. Forest fires also kill trees and weaken soil.

The U.S. Geological Survey identifies areas at risk for landslides. The information they collect can be used by land owners and governments to watch, and sometimes evacuate, dangerous hillsides.

Landslide Disaster!

Fill in the circle next to the correct answer.

1. Which of the following can cause a landslide?

   (A) ash from a volcano

   (B) earthquake

   (C) heavy rain

   (D) all of the above

2. "To leave quickly" means the same as _____ .

   (A) erosion

   (B) erupt

   (C) evacuate

   (D) entire

3. Which of the following can help to prevent landslides?

   (A) listening to expert predictions and adding loose rocks to the hill

   (B) planting trees and grasses on the hill

   (C) adding clay to the soil and removing trees

   (D) drying out the hillside and building houses

4. Where is a mudslide most likely to occur?

   (A) in the desert

   (B) in the mountains

   (C) on the prairies

   (D) on the savannah

5. List three things that can happen after a landslide.

   _____

   _____

   _____

Landslide Disaster!

Complete the cause/effect chart below.

Causes of a Landslide	Effects of a Landslide

WRITING Research another natural occurrence, such as a volcanic eruption, hurricane, or earthquake. Create a cause/effect chart for it.

MASON, BRIDGET "BIDDY" (1818-1891)

Bridget "Biddy" Mason, a former slave who became wealthy and used her money to help the poor.

YEARS UNDER SLAVERY

Bridget "Biddy" Mason was born into slavery in the early 1800s. She grew up on a Mississippi plantation owned by Robert Smith. Because she was enslaved, Biddy was forbidden to learn to read or write.

In 1847, Smith moved his household to Utah. Four years later, Smith moved everyone again, this time to California. During both journeys, Mason had to walk behind the wagons, keeping watch to see that the farm animals did not run off.

THE ROAD TO FREEDOM

When the group reached California, Smith found out that California did not allow slavery. Smith then tried to move his 14 enslaved workers out of the state. Local African Americans took him to court to prevent this.

Mason was not allowed to speak in court, but she told her story to the judge in private. In 1856, all of Smith's enslaved workers won their freedom.

LIFE IN LOS ANGELES

Biddy Mason settled in Los Angeles where she became a nurse. She helped hundreds of families, rich and poor, black and white.

Ten years after gaining her freedom, Mason bought land just outside of town for $250. She was

The deed shows ownership of the land Biddy Mason purchased in 1866.

one of the first African-American women to own land in Los Angeles. As the city of Los Angeles grew, Mason's land became very valuable. She bought more property and became very wealthy.

Mason used her money to help the poor of all races. She gave generously to charities and provided food and shelter for the poor. Her home was known as the House of the Open Hand. During the great flood of 1861-1862 and the two-year drought that followed, Biddy Mason allowed flood victims to use her account at a local grocery store. Even on the day she died, there were needy people outside her door.

BIDDY MASON REMEMBERED

Biddy Mason was buried in an unmarked grave. Almost 100 years later, the mayor of Los Angeles led a ceremony to place a tombstone on her grave.

November 16, 1989 was declared Biddy Mason Day. A memorial of her achievements was built in downtown Los Angeles. It is in the park that bears her name.

See also LOS ANGELES HISTORY.

FACT FILE
Slave or Free States?

- Before the Civil War, there was a great deal of conflict over whether new states would be admitted to the union as slave states, allowing slavery, or free states, not allowing slavery.

- In 1850, California joined the union as a free state. Therefore, slavery was against the law in California.

Biddy Mason

Fill in the circle next to the correct answer.

1. Biddy Mason was given her freedom because _____ .

   (A) Smith thought slavery was wrong

   (B) slavery was against the law in California

   (C) she had enough money to buy her freedom

   (D) her owner, Robert Smith, died

2. Why do you think Mason's home was known as the House of the Open Hand?

   (A) People gave Mason money there.

   (B) The Masons were poor.

   (C) It was on Hand Street.

   (D) People could go there and get help.

3. The headings in the article tell you _____ .

   (A) who the article is about

   (B) the main idea of each section

   (C) details about each section

   (D) why the person is important

4. Put a check mark (✔) in front of the words that best describe Biddy Mason.

   ___ generous   ___ businesswoman

   ___ determined   ___ artistic

   ___ afraid   ___ caring

5. The text structure of the article is sequence. Circle the signal words in the article that show the text structure. Remember to include time phrases as well as dates.

Biddy Mason

Use the graphic organizer below to create a time line of the important events in the life of Biddy Mason. Write the event that matches the given date. Add any other dates that you think are important.

DATE   EVENT

1818 _____
       _____
       _____

1851 _____
       _____

1856 _____
       _____
       _____

1866 _____
       _____
       _____

1891 _____
       _____
       _____

WRITING Why do you think Biddy Mason is still remembered today? Support your opinion with facts about her life.

Mister Mom

Animal Dads Bring Up Babies in Some Unusual Ways

By Emily Costello

Yellowhead jawfish

Lots of kids have dads that stay home to care for the family. Likewise, some wild animal dads go the extra mile to keep their babies safe.

Take the yellowhead jawfish shown here. Dad's babies, still at the beginning of their **life cycle,** would be an easy target for hungry predators. To protect their offspring, this proud papa pops his growing eggs into his mouth. The 10-centimeter-long (4-inch) fish can cradle about 500 eggs in his mouth for up to a week. When Daddy's stomach grumbles, he digs a hole in the sand below the coral reefs. There he hides the eggs. This frees up Dad's mouth so he can grab a quick snack.

Animal dads do what comes naturally, explains Dario Maestripieri, a professor as the University of Chicago. "Some animals have instincts that tell them to be good parents," she says. The result: Their babies are likely to survive and pass their parents' genes (jeens) on to their own offspring.

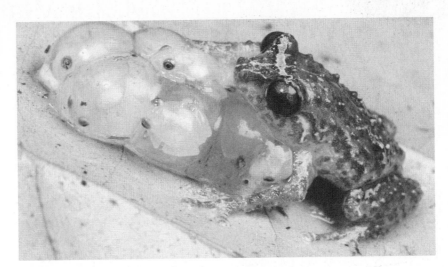

Oreophryne frogs

Piggyback Rides

The male giant water bug may be the insect world's best dad. This 2.5-centimeter-long (1-inch) bug allows his mate to "glue" about 150 eggs to his wings with a sticky foam. Dad does underwater "pushups" to move fresh water over the soft-shelled eggs. The water keeps the eggs moist and allows them to "breathe." Hiding from hungry birds becomes a challenge for Daddy: The eggs on his back triple in size before hatching.

Dad on Duty

Like many new dads, Oreophryne (OR-ee-oh-frine) frogs don't get much sleep. After the female lays her eggs on the quiet underside of a leaf, the male spends nights guarding the eggs and keeping them moist. Most frogs hatch as tadpoles in fresh water and go through **metamorphosis** (met-tuh-MOR-fuh-sis) to become adults. But Oreophryne frogs are born as mini-adults called froglets. This allows them to grow up far from water—a good thing since their New Guinea home experiences frequent deadly flash floods.

Daddy Dearest

A female dwarf seahorse squirts her eggs into a pouch in her mate's belly. The pregnant male carries the developing, or growing, eggs for several weeks. His safe and cozy pouch provides oxygen and removes waste for the eggs. After about two weeks, he gives birth to up to 30 teeny babies. Not bad for a fish that tops out at 3.8 centimeters (1.5 inches)! The babies look like mini versions of their parents. This *direct development* means they're born bigger than their neighbors that hatch from eggs. So predators like crabs and eels are less likely to gobble up the seahorses. Also, **camouflage** (CA-muh-flahj) helps them blend with their seagrass home.

Dwarf seahorse

Mister Mom

Fill in the circle next to the correct answer.

1. Why do animals put so much effort into raising their offspring?

   Ⓐ to scare competition from taking their homes

   Ⓑ so their babies survive to pass on their genes

   Ⓒ to attract a mate later in life

   Ⓓ to keep their babies clean and well-fed

2. Which is <u>not</u> a stage in an animal's life cycle?

   Ⓐ birth

   Ⓑ development

   Ⓒ camouflage

   Ⓓ death

3. A *predator* is another name for an _____ .

   Ⓐ animal's baby

   Ⓑ animal dad

   Ⓒ animal's enemy

   Ⓓ adult animal

4. Which animal dad takes care of the most babies?

   Ⓐ giant water bug

   Ⓑ dwarf seahorse

   Ⓒ Oreophryne frog

   Ⓓ yellowhead jawfish

5. <u>Underline</u> the sentences that explain each animal dad's job in raising its offspring. Then write what human dads do to help raise their children.

   _____

   _____

   _____

Mister Mom

Record the key characteristics of each animal dad. Be sure to include the role each dad plays in its children's lives.

Animal Dad   *Characteristics*

yellowhead jawfish

* _____

* _____

* _____

giant water bug

* _____

* _____

* _____

Oreophryne frog

* _____

* _____

* _____

dwarf seahorse

* _____

* _____

* _____

WRITING Find out about other animal dads. You may wish to research emperor penguins, ring-tailed lemurs, or another animal of your choice. Create a fact card about the animal dad. On one side paste or draw a picture. On the other side, explain how the animal dad helps to raise its children.

MONARCHS TAKE FLIGHT

WORD WISE

climate The kind of weather that a place usually has.

generations The children, grandchildren, great grand-children, and so on of a person or animal.

migrate To move from one climate to another, when the season changes.

offspring A person's or an animal's young.

TIP: As you read, look for signal words, such as months of the year, that will help you follow the sequence of events.

ON THE MOVE Every fall, in September and October, millions of monarch butterflies of North America begin flying south to warmer **climates**. Monarch butterflies that start out from places west of the Rocky Mountains head for California. Those starting from places east of the Rocky Mountains head for Mexico.

In all the world, no other butterflies **migrate** like the monarch butterflies of North America. Huge groups of monarch butterflies travel up to three thousand miles. Weighing less than a paper clip, monarch butterflies can travel 50 to 80 miles a day.

Rest is very important on such a long trip. The monarch butterflies have stopping points along the way. Groups of butterflies often cluster in trees at night to rest. During the day, they stop to feed on flower nectar.

DESTINATION HOME The monarch butterflies that survive the long trip and are not eaten by birds finally arrive at the places in Mexico where they will spend the winter months. They cluster together in trees that protect them from rain and wind. Often they cover whole tree trunks and branches.

Then in March, as winter ends, they begin the long trip back north. When the female butterflies reach the southern part of the United States, they look for milkweed plants on which to lay their eggs. Milkweed leaves are the only things the newly hatched insect can eat. The female butterflies live just long enough to lay their eggs. Soon, their **offspring** develop into full-grown butterflies and continue the journey north to their parents' original home. Over the summer, the female offspring will lay hundreds of eggs, and new **generations** of monarch butterflies will grow. The new butterflies will be the grandchildren and great-grandchildren and great-great grandchildren of the monarch butterflies that went south the previous fall. It takes up to three generations to complete one year's migration.

In September and October, the newest generation of monarch butterflies will begin the trip south. Amazingly, they fly to the very same places, and often the very same trees, as the monarch butterflies that lived before them!

Monarch butterflies nest on tree trunks when they arrive at their winter homes. Here, thousands of butterflies cover a tree.

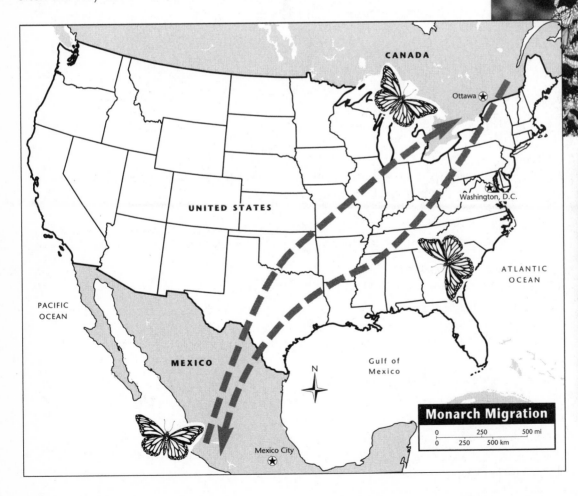

CANADA

Ottawa ✪

UNITED STATES

Washington, D.C. ✪

ATLANTIC OCEAN

PACIFIC OCEAN

MEXICO

N

Gulf of Mexico

Mexico City ✪

Monarch Migration

| 0 | 250 | 500 mi |
| 0 | 250 | 500 km |

Monarchs Take Flight

Fill in the circle next to the correct answer.

1. Why do monarch butterflies migrate in the fall?

   (A) to escape cold weather

   (B) to lay eggs

   (C) to find new sources of food

   (D) to escape from enemies, such as birds

2. A word that is related to *migrate* is

   (A) migration

   (B) immigration

   (C) immigrant

   (D) all of the above

3. The monarch butterflies that wintered in Mexico travel _____ in the spring.

   (A) northwest

   (B) northeast

   (C) southwest

   (D) southeast

4. Circle or highlight the words in "Monarchs Take Flight" that clued you in to the sequence of the monarch butterflies' flight.

5. What information in the article did you find most amazing?

   _____

   _____

   _____

An Incredible Journey

The map shows the path of monarch butterflies as they migrate south and then back up north over a year's time. Fill in the sequence of their journey. On each numbered line, write the season or the months when the butterflies are in that location.

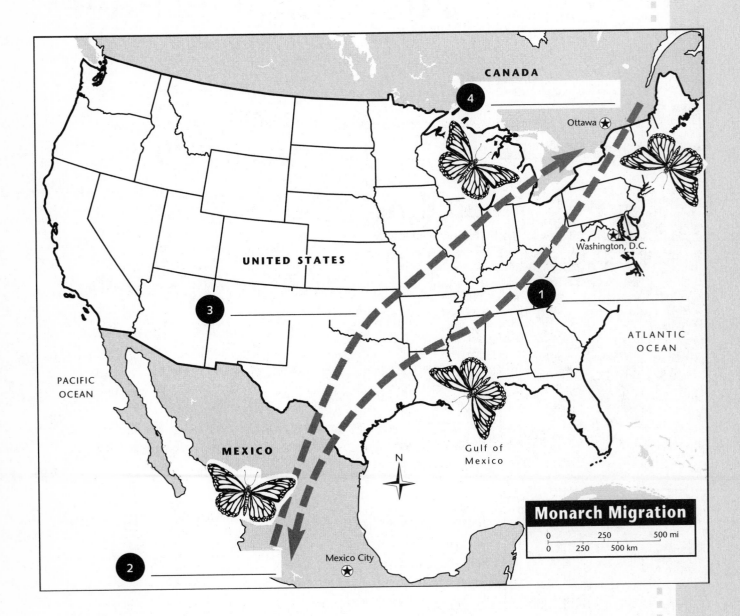

![pencil icon] **WRITING** Write a short summary of the monarch butterflies' migration. Be sure to cover all the seasons in a year. Your summary should begin with what happens in the fall and end with the following summer.

WORD WISE

amateur Someone who takes part in a sport or other activity for pleasure rather than for money.

boycott To refuse to buy something or take part in something as a way to protest.

chronic Something that does not get better for a long time.

patent A legal document giving the inventor of some item sole rights to make or sell the item.

¡Celebrate Hispanic Heritage!

Born 1901-1949

César Chávez
Union Leader
Mexican American
1927–1993

César Chávez came from a family of poor migrant workers. Through the experiences of his family, he knew the hard lives led by farm workers who came to work in California from Mexico. They had to live in dirty, cramped places and earned little money. In 1962, with Dolores Huerta, he started a group to change these terrible conditions—the United Farm Workers of America. At first the workers were afraid of the produce growers. But Chávez inspired the group and led peaceful protests and **boycotts**. These actions convinced the growers to sign contracts with the farm workers and to treat them better.

Jaime Escalante
Teacher
Bolivian American
Born 1930

Jaime Escalante is a teacher who has changed the lives of Latino students in poor neighborhoods in Los Angeles. When he first came to Garfield High School, many of his students were failing. Escalante fought for better textbooks and inspired his students to succeed by setting high standards and winning over his tough students. The movie *Stand and Deliver* is about how his students proved they could succeed by passing a very difficult math test before college.

Roberto Clemente
Major League Baseball Player
Puerto Rican
1934–1972
Proud of his Puerto Rican roots, Roberto Clemente drew attention to the excellence of Latin American players in Major League baseball during the 1960s and early 1970s. A player for the Pittsburgh Pirates, he was the first Puerto Rican to be voted Most Valuable Player. A great fielder and hitter, Clemente was loved by many because of his deep concern for people and work on behalf of his native Puerto Ricans. Clemente was killed in a plane crash on his way to take supplies to earthquake victims in Nicaragua on New Year's Eve 1972. He was elected to the Baseball Hall of Fame in 1973.

Antonia C. Novello
Doctor, Former United States Surgeon General
Puerto Rican
Born 1944
In 1990, Antonia Novello became the first Hispanic person—and the first woman as well—to be appointed as Surgeon General, the chief doctor in the United States. As a child, she had a **chronic** illness that hurt her digestion, causing her great suffering. She never forgot that experience. As surgeon general, Novello especially campaigned for better care for children. She also paid special attention to the problems of alcoholism, smoking, AIDS, and violence.

Born 1950 and After

Franklin R. Chang-Díaz
Astronaut
Costa Rican American
Born 1950
Raised in a poor family in Costa Rica, Franklin Chang-Díaz studied hard to become a scientist. He also became a U.S. citizen. Chang-Díaz was the first Hispanic person to enter the space program, becoming an astronaut in 1981. He is a veteran of six space missions and has spent nearly 1,300 hours in space.

Nancy Lopez
Professional Golfer
Mexican American
Born 1957

Nancy Lopez is one of the greatest women golfers of all time. She had an early start at greatness—she began to play golf at age 8. She was only 12 when she won the New Mexico Women's **Amateur** tournament. One of the top pro-golf money winners of all time, Lopez has won 48 titles. In 1989, she was inducted into the PGA World Golf Hall of Fame.

Gloria Estefan
Singer and Musician
Cuban American
Born 1957

Gloria Estefan has been loved and admired by people throughout the world not only for her music, but for her bravery in the face of difficulties. Born in Cuba, Estefan came to Miami, Florida, as a young child when her parents fled the Communist government of Fidel Castro. In the late 1970s, she became a singer with the group Miami Sound Machine. The group became very famous. Estefan won awards for her music and for her work on causes such as campaigning against drugs. In 1990, a terrible accident occurred. Estefan and her family were traveling in their bus when it was hit by a truck. The singer suffered serious injuries. Through patience, hard work, and good fortune, however, she was able to recover fully and return to the stage. Her music remains appreciated by millions of listeners.

Ellen Ochoa
Astronaut
Mexican American
Born 1958

Ellen Ochoa was the first Hispanic woman to become an astronaut. A veteran of two space flights, she first flew in space on the shuttle *Discovery* in 1993. Sally Ride, the first woman astronaut in the U.S., was one of her role models. Ochoa is not only an astronaut but also an inventor, holding three **patents**. When she is in space, she says that she loves "looking out the window at the Earth."

¡Celebrate Hispanic Heritage!

Fill in the circle next to the correct answer.

1. How is the article organized?

   Ⓐ People from the same country appear on the same page.

   Ⓑ People with similar jobs are grouped together.

   Ⓒ People who were born in the same time period are together.

   Ⓓ People are arranged in alphabetical order.

2. Which person was <u>not</u> born before 1950?

   Ⓐ César Chávez

   Ⓑ Antonia Novello

   Ⓒ Ellen Ochoa

   Ⓓ Roberto Clemente

3. What do Franklin Chang-Díaz and Ellen Ochoa have in common?

   Ⓐ both are from Costa Rica

   Ⓑ both were born in 1950

   Ⓒ both are inventors

   Ⓓ both have flown in space

4. Who else might you find in this article?

   Ⓐ former president, Bill Clinton

   Ⓑ astronaut, Sally Ride

   Ⓒ singer, Ricky Martin

   Ⓓ TV personality, Oprah Winfrey

5. Select one person in the article that you admire. Write what this person accomplished and why you admire him or her.

   _____

   _____

¡Celebrate Hispanic Heritage!

List five people from the article. Record three facts about each person.

1. Person's Name

    _____

Facts Learned

✴ _____

✴ _____

✴ _____

2. Person's Name

    _____

Facts Learned

✴ _____

✴ _____

✴ _____

3. Person's Name

    _____

Facts Learned

✴ _____

✴ _____

✴ _____

4. Person's Name

    _____

Facts Learned

✴ _____

✴ _____

✴ _____

5. Person's Name

    _____

Facts Learned

✴ _____

✴ _____

✴ _____

WRITING Research famous Asian Americans. Go to teacher.scholastic.com/activities/asian-american/notables.htm. Select one person and write a brief article.

Drip, Drop, Drip!

THE WATER CYCLE

The water on Earth is never used up. It just keeps going round and round in a cycle we call the water cycle. Water moves constantly from oceans, rivers, and lakes into the air, then back to the earth, and then into the air again.

Because of this cycle, there is as much water on Earth today as there ever was—or ever will be. Water only changes from one form to another and moves from one place to another. The glass of water you drank yesterday may have been flowing in Egypt's Nile River two thousand years ago.

109

EVAPORATION AND TRANSPIRATION

The sun's heat evaporates water. Water rises into the air as an invisible gas called **vapor**. This is what happens, for example, if you hang a wet shirt on a clothesline to dry. The shirt dries as the water evaporates. About 85% of the water vapor in the air comes from oceans and seas, which cover almost three-quarters of the earth's surface. (See diagram #1.)

But plants and trees also add moisture. After plants have drawn water from the ground through their roots, they pass some of it out through their leaves in a process called **transpiration.** The leaves of a birch tree, for example, can give off 70 gallons of water a day! So while plants and trees depend on the water cycle to live, they also add to it.

READING TIP

Stop and study the cycle diagram. Notice that the arrows go from one step to the next without end. That's because a cycle never ends.

• Go from the number in the text to the same number in the diagram.

• Read the explanation and look at the illustration.

• Then go back to where you left off in the text.

WATER VAPOR INTO RAIN

As the invisible water vapor rises into the air, it cools and forms a cloud. The air is moving around all the time, however. If it pushes a cloud high up into the atmosphere, the cloud will cool further. Cool air cannot hold as much water vapor as warm air, so tiny drops of water will **condense**, or form in the cloud. They fall to the earth as rain, or as hail or snow if they are frozen. (See diagram #2.)

The rain or snow adds water to rivers, lakes, and streams. The water seeps into the ground. (See diagram #3.) Over time, rivers and streams carry the water back to the oceans. And the water cycle continues. (See diagram #4.)

The Water Cycle

Fill in the circle next to the correct answer.

1. Which statement is true?

    (A) A cycle keeps repeating itself without an end.

    (B) A cycle goes from one step to another until it is finished.

    (C) A cycle lasts only for a short time.

    (D) Every cycle has four steps.

2. Which of the following could be shown in a cycle diagram?

    (A) the making of an automobile

    (B) the seasons

    (C) a day at school

    (D) a baseball game

3. Water vapor is _____ .

    (A) a solid

    (B) a liquid

    (C) a gas

    (D) ice

4. When will the water cycle end?

    (A) in about a thousand years

    (B) when there is a drought

    (C) in the next century

    (D) never

5. Why does most of the water in the air come from oceans and seas?

    _____

    _____

    _____

The Water Cycle

Fill in the cycle diagram to show the four main steps in the sequence of the water cycle. Reread the article to figure out what they are.

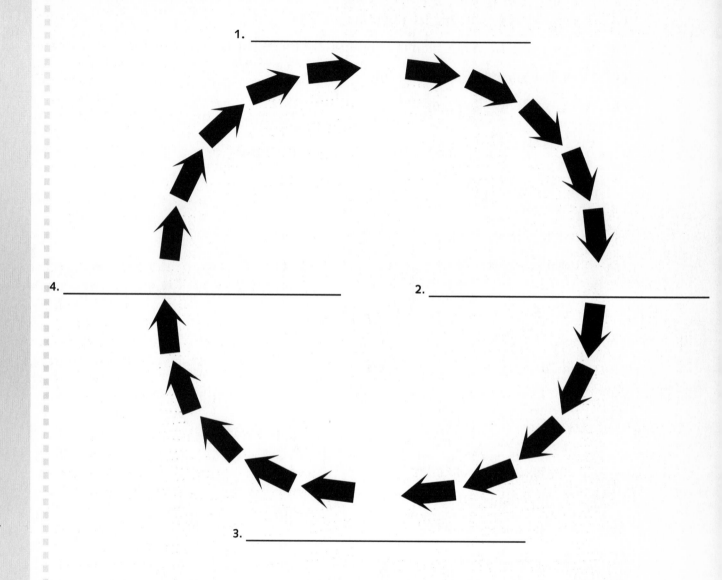

1. _____

2. _____

3. _____

4. _____

WRITING Write a short explanation of the water cycle. Use your graphic organizer to help you put the steps in the right order.

Breaking Barriers

It may be hard to imagine, but in 1945 there wasn't a single African-American player in professional baseball, football, or basketball. Outside of sports, life was also segregated. In the South, there were "Jim Crow" laws that set up separate schools, restaurants, hotels, bathrooms, buses, and even water fountains for blacks and whites. But a man named Jackie Robinson was about to take a giant step forward. In 1945, he was the first African-American man to play baseball in the Major Leagues. What did it take to make this happen?

Read about how Jackie Robinson helped solve the problem of injustice in sports. And find out about some of the people who helped him.

The nine values below guided Jackie Robinson on and off the field and helped him break barriers in both sports and life.

1 **Courage** When Branch Rickey, president of the Brooklyn Dodgers ball club, met with Jackie Robinson, he said that he wanted a "player with guts enough not to fight back." Robinson agreed. While breaking the color barrier in baseball, Jackie had to face racism and insults as he excelled on the field. His courage and talent opened doors in all sports for others to follow.

2 **Determination** On their way to spring training, Jackie and his wife, Rachel, were bumped from three different airplanes. Their seats were given to white people. They finally got on a bus, but they were forced to sit in the back. These were the kinds of indignities that African Americans in the South suffered regularly during that time, and Jackie had to practice determination to keep working toward his goals.

3 **Teamwork** Jackie and his teammates often faced hostile crowds. Pee Wee Reese, one of Jackie's white teammates, had a simple response. He walked over to Jackie and put his hand on his shoulder. Together they sent a clear message to racists: We believe in teamwork. We came here to play.

WORD WISE

barriers (BA-ree-ur) Something that blocks the way.

determination (di-tur-mi-NAY-shun) The will to do something; courage.

integrity (in-TEG-ruh-tee) honest; sticking to what one believes is right.

persistence (pur-SIS-tinse) Continuing to try to do something even if there are difficulties.

4 **Persistence** The Dodgers were a great team who had been to the World Series often, but had never won. In the first game of the 1955 World Series, the Dodgers were losing. Jackie decided to shake things up by stealing home. This gave his team new energy. They persisted and went on to win their first World Series.

5 **Integrity** When Jackie announced his retirement from baseball, he took a job in the business world. Then, another baseball team offered him a lot of money to play for them. Reporters predicted that Jackie would go for the money. Instead, he stayed with the business. From this action, everyone learned that he had integrity and wouldn't go back on a promise.

6 **Citizenship** When the Robinson family had dinner, they didn't talk about baseball. They talked about wrongs happening in the world and what they could do to make a change. The children grew up knowing that, as citizens, they had a responsibility to try to make the world a better place.

7 **Justice** "A life is not important except in the impact it has on other lives," Jackie once wrote. Even after he became successful, he was never satisfied knowing that others were denied basic civil rights. Throughout his life, Jackie practiced justice by seeing that all people were treated fairly, no matter who they were.

8 **Commitment** Commitment is tested when times are tough. The Robinson family experienced this when Jackie Jr., the oldest son, became addicted to drugs and landed in jail. His family saw him through treatment and recovery. But just as he was turning his life around, he was killed in a car accident. His family members' commitment to one another got them through that difficult time.

9 **Excellence** Excellence is the result of combining Jackie's other values and putting them into practice. By holding yourself to a high standard, you can achieve your goals—just like Jackie did.

Breaking Barriers

Fill in the circle next to the correct answer.

1. Jackie Robinson's goal was _____ .

   (A) to become a famous baseball player

   (B) to end racism in the South

   (C) to end racism in baseball

   (D) to become a businessman

2. Pee Wee Reese showed hostile crowds that he _____ .

   (A) supported Jackie Robinson

   (B) was a great player

   (C) wanted to play on another team

   (D) was jealous of Jackie Robinson

3. Jackie Robinson had *integrity*, so people knew that he would _____ .

   (A) keep his word once he had given it

   (B) change his mind if he needed to

   (C) go back on a promise he had made

   (D) keep playing baseball

4. Which of the following is an example of persistence on the ice skating rink?

   (A) It was cold out, so Jack decided not to go ice skating.

   (B) Even though Emily kept falling down, she got up and tried again.

   (C) Alex kept falling on the ice, so he took off his skates and went home.

   (D) Donna helped her younger brother by holding his hand.

5. What did Branch Rickey mean when he said that he wanted a player with the courage "not to fight back"?

   _____

   _____

   _____

Breaking Barriers

The article "Breaking Barriers" was about the problems caused by injustice and some of the people who had the courage to try to find solutions. For each problem, write an example of who took steps to solve it and how.

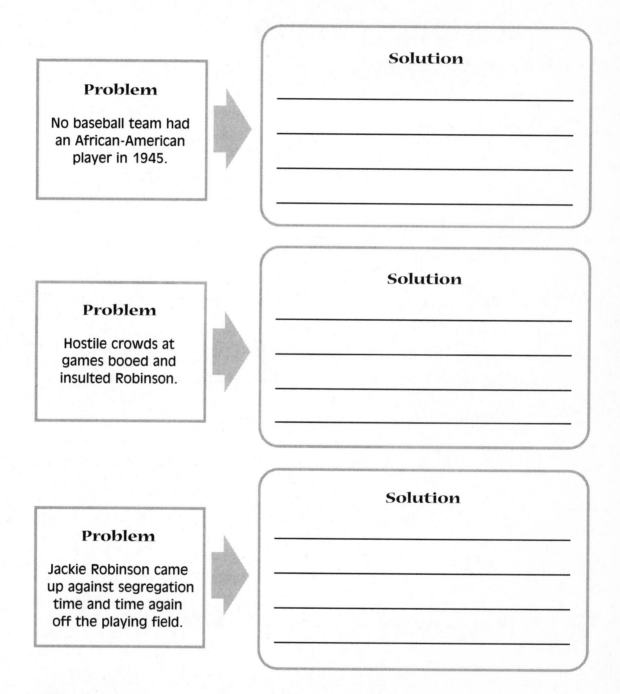

Solution
_____
_____
_____
_____

Problem

No baseball team had an African-American player in 1945.

Solution
_____
_____
_____
_____

Problem

Hostile crowds at games booed and insulted Robinson.

Solution
_____
_____
_____
_____

Problem

Jackie Robinson came up against segregation time and time again off the playing field.

WRITING Choose three of the values that guided Jackie Robinson. Give an example of a time when you or someone you know has shown each of the characteristics you chose.

Imagine trekking through a land where temperatures dip below -100°F, winds are more than 200 miles an hour, and whiteouts make everything around you seem like the inside of a ping-pong ball! Although this description may sound unpleasant, **Antarctica** attracts many explorers and scientists.

AT THE BOTTOM OF THE WORLD

Exploring Antarctica

Atlantic Ocean

Indian Ocean

ANTARCTICA
◆ South Pole

ANTARCTICA

Pacific Ocean

These two scientists are holding ice collected from a deep snow pit. The stacks of snow around them came from the same pit.

FACT FILE
Antarctica

* is the coldest, windiest continent.
* is as large as the United States and Mexico combined.
* has no native human population.
* contains 70% of the planet's freshwater in the form of glaciers.
* has freezing temperatures all year long that keep anything from rotting.
* has ice up to three miles thick.
* is surrounded by 93% of the world's icebergs.

This is one of the many icebergs found in the seas around Antarctica. A well-known iceberg, named B-10A, is bigger than the state of Rhode Island. ▼

Working at the Bottom of the World

Denise Hardesty's job is for the birds. That's because she spends her winters living among thousands of penguins that make their home in the frozen wilderness of Antarctica.

Hardesty is one of more than 300 women working at Antarctica's McMurdo Station, a science research program run by the National Science Foundation.

Thirty-five years ago, people thought that women like Hardesty were not strong enough to brave Antarctica's **frigid**, or freezing-cold, climate. But finally, in 1969, the first American female scientists joined the U.S. Antarctic program. Today women at McMurdo operate bulldozers and pilot helicopters. They work as carpenters and electricians. They dive beneath the frozen ocean and explore Antarctica's skies. They also supervise research labs and survival training.

Scientists drill a hole through the thick ice to study how fish have adapted to cold water. ▼

Survival on the Ice

Hardesty works during Antarctica's summer season, which stretches from late December through late March. The sun shines 24 hours a day. Temperatures in the summer remain in the teens, but that's warm compared to winter temperatures. In 1963, Antarctica recorded a world-record low temperature of -129°F!

Even though the summer makes it possible for scientists to work outside, Antarctica's weather can still be unpredictable. Hardesty never leaves home without gear for extreme weather—goggles, facemask, mittens, long underwear, parka, and boots.

Because of the harsh climate, attending survival training is **mandatory**, or required.

The Weddell seal is the only mammal that lives on Antarctica's ice and in its cold waters all year long. A 3-day-old seal pup stays close to its resting mother. ▼

The students learn how to build emergency shelters, rescue team members, and operate communications equipment.

Knowing your limits and how to survive is critical down here, where the weather is extreme enough to kill a person in a matter of hours," says Hardesty.

Project Penguins

Hardesty spends most of her time in Antarctica working in the field, where home is a one-person tent. Work means hanging out with more than 7,000 penguins.

Now in her second season on "the Ice," Hardesty is studying how penguins reproduce and care for their young. She spends her days counting and weighing chicks, studying their diets, and observing their behavior.

Antarctica is home to more than 100 million penguins, so Hardesty has lots of subjects to observe! One of her subjects is the emperor penguin.

Emperor Penguins

Emperor penguins are the largest of the penguin species. They are nearly four feet tall and weigh up to 90 pounds. Emperor penguins spend their entire lives on the cold Antarctic ice and in the icy waters that surround it.

In winter, which comes to Antarctica in March, the female emperor penguin lays one egg. Then she goes into the water to feed. What happens to the egg? The male emperor penguin takes care of it. He balances the egg on the tops of his feet, covering it with his pouch (a warm layer of skin) for warmth. Each male stands with the egg on his feet for about two months, through ice-cold days and nights, freezing winds, and blizzards. The males eat nothing that whole time.

To keep warm, the males huddle together tightly in a large group. They take turns moving into the center of the group, where it's warmer because it's protected from the icy winds. Once the males in the center warm up, they shuffle back to the outside of the group, giving their fellow penguins a turn in the center. All this is done with the egg on their feet!

After about two months, the baby penguins, called chicks, hatch. Finally, the females return from the sea, bringing food for the chicks. Now it's the turn of the hungry males to go to sea for food.

As the young penguins grow, the males and females take turns going back and forth to sea to bring back food for them. By December, the chicks are old enough to take to the water and fish for their own food. And Denise Hardesty is right there to study them. ❄

Scientists can study penguins up close because the penguins aren't afraid of humans. ▼

An Emperor penguin egg rests on the feet of the father penguin.
◀

An Emperor penguin keeps its newly-hatched chick warm.
◀

At the Bottom of the World

Fill in the circle next to the correct answer.

1. Denise Hardesty works as a _____ .

   Ⓐ helicopter pilot

   Ⓑ travel writer

   Ⓒ research scientist

   Ⓓ bulldozer operator

2. Which of the following is <u>not</u> something the researchers learned during survival training?

   Ⓐ how to save other team members caught in a snowstorm

   Ⓑ how to make emergency shelters when far from the lab

   Ⓒ how to work special communication gadgets

   Ⓓ how to safely follow large groups of Emperor penguins

3. Another word for "extremely cold" is _____ .

   Ⓐ balmy

   Ⓑ blizzard

   Ⓒ frigid

   Ⓓ unpleasant

4. Which of the following words best describes the role of a male Emperor penguin?

   Ⓐ difficult

   Ⓑ critical

   Ⓒ caring

   Ⓓ all of the above

5. <u>Underline</u> five facts in the article that tell about the male Emperor penguin.

Antarctica Data Sheet

For each topic below, write three facts from the article.

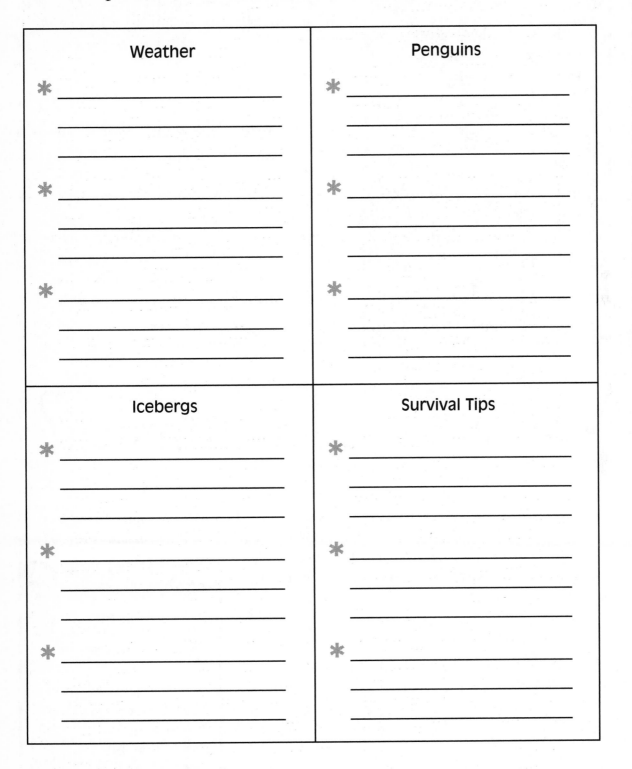

Weather

* _____

_____

* _____

_____

_____

* _____

_____

Penguins

* _____

_____

* _____

_____

_____

* _____

_____

Icebergs

* _____

_____

* _____

_____

_____

* _____

_____

Survival Tips

* _____

_____

_____

* _____

_____

* _____

_____

WRITING Do research about other Antarctic penguins such as chinstrap, Adélie, and gentoos. Write up your findings in a fact file.

Detail from a mural on the wall of a Pompeian home

ON AUGUST 24, 79 A.D. MOUNT VESUVIUS LITERALLY BLEW ITS TOP, SPEWING TONS OF MOLTEN ASH, PUMICE, AND SULFURIC GAS MILES INTO THE ATMOSPHERE. A "FIRESTORM" OF POISONOUS VAPORS AND MOLTEN DEBRIS ENGULFED THE SURROUNDING AREA SUFFOCATING THE INHABITANTS OF THE NEIGHBORING ROMAN RESORT CITIES OF POMPEII, HERCULANEUM, AND STABIAE. TONS OF FALLING DEBRIS FILLED THE STREETS UNTIL NOTHING REMAINED TO BE SEEN OF THE ONCE THRIVING COMMUNITIES. THE CITIES REMAINED BURIED AND UNDISCOVERED FOR ALMOST 1500 YEARS UNTIL EXCAVATION BEGAN IN 1748. THESE EXCAVATIONS CONTINUE TODAY AND PROVIDE INSIGHT INTO LIFE DURING THE ROMAN EMPIRE.

AN ANCIENT VOICE REACHES OUT FROM THE PAST TO TELL US OF THE DISASTER. THIS VOICE BELONGS TO PLINY THE YOUNGER WHOSE LETTERS DESCRIBE HIS EXPERIENCE DURING THE ERUPTION WHILE HE WAS STAYING IN THE HOME OF HIS UNCLE, PLINY THE ELDER. THE ELDER PLINY WAS AN OFFICIAL IN THE ROMAN COURT, IN CHARGE OF THE FLEET IN THE AREA OF THE BAY OF NAPLES AND A NATURALIST. PLINY THE YOUNGER'S LETTERS WERE DISCOVERED IN THE 16TH CENTURY.

What's Buried at Pompeii?

Wrath of the Gods

A few years after the event, Pliny wrote to a friend, Cornelius Tacitus, describing the happenings of late August 79 A.D. when the eruption of Vesuvius obliterated Pompeii, killed his uncle and almost destroyed his family. At the time, Pliny was eighteen and living at his uncle's villa in the town of Misenum. We pick up his story as he describes the warning raised by his mother:

My uncle was stationed at Misenum, in active command of the fleet. On 24 August, in the early afternoon, my mother drew his attention to a cloud of unusual size and appearance. He had been out in the sun, had taken a cold bath, and lunched while lying down, and was then working at his books. He called for his shoes and climbed up to a place which would give him the best view of the phenomenon. It was not clear at that distance from which mountain the cloud was rising (it was afterwards known to be Vesuvius); its general appearance can best be expressed as being like an umbrella pine, for it rose to a great height on

WORD WISE

This guide will help you with words in the article that you may not know how to pronounce.

debris (duh-BREE)

phenomenon (fe-NOM-uh-non)

Pliny (PLIN-ee)

Pompeii (pom-PAY)

pumice (PUHM-iss)

spew (spyoo)

Vesuvius (veh-SOO-vee-us)

a sort of trunk and then split off into branches, I imagine because it was thrust upwards by the first blast and then left unsupported as the pressure subsided, or else it was borne down by its own weight so that it spread out and gradually dispersed. In places it looked white, elsewhere blotched and dirty, according to the amount of soil and ashes it carried with it.

My uncle's scholarly acumen saw at once that it was important enough for a closer inspection, and he ordered a boat to be made ready, telling me I could come with him if I wished. I replied that I preferred to go on with my studies, and as it happened he had himself given me some writing to do. As he was leaving the house he was handed a message from Rectina, wife of Tascus whose house was at the foot of the mountain, so that escape was impossible except by boat. She was terrified by the danger threatening her and implored him to rescue her from her fate. He changed his plans, and what he had begun in a spirit of inquiry he completed as a hero. He gave orders for the warships to be launched and went on board himself with the intention of bringing help to many more people besides Rectina, for this lovely stretch of coast was thickly populated.

He hurried to the place which everyone else was hastily leaving, steering his course straight for the danger zone. He was entirely fearless, describing each new movement and phase of the portent to be noted down exactly as he observed them. Ashes were already falling, hotter and thicker as the ships drew near, followed by bits of pumice and blackened stones, charred and cracked by the flames: then suddenly they were in shallow water, and the shore was blocked by the debris from the mountain.

For a moment my uncle wondered whether to turn back, but when the helmsman advised this he refused, telling him that Fortune stood by the courageous and they must make for Pomponianus at Stabiae. He was cut off there by the breadth of the bay (for the shore gradually curves round a basin filled by the sea) so that he was not as yet in danger, though it was clear that this would come nearer as it spread. Pomponianus had therefore already put his belongings on board ship, intending to escape if the contrary wind fell. This wind was of course full in my uncle's favor, and he was able to bring his ship in. He embraced his terrified friend, cheered and encouraged him, and thinking he could calm his fears by showing his own composure, gave orders that he was to be carried to the bathroom. After his bath he lay down and dined; he was quite cheerful, or at any rate he pretended he was, which was no less courageous.

Vesuvius erupts in 1944

Meanwhile on Mount Vesuvius broad sheets of fire and leaping flames blazed at several points, their bright glare emphasized by the darkness of night. My uncle tried to allay the fears of his companions by repeatedly declaring that these were nothing but bonfires left by the peasants in their terror, or else empty houses on fire in the districts they had abandoned. Then he went to rest and certainly slept, for as he was a stout man his breathing was rather loud and heavy and could be heard by people coming and going outside his door. By this time the courtyard giving access to his room was full of ashes mixed with pumice stones, so that its level had risen, and if he had stayed in the room any longer he would never have got out. He was wakened, came out and joined Pomponianus and the rest of the household who had sat up all night.

They debated whether to stay indoors or take their chance in the open, for the buildings were now shaking with violent shocks, and seemed to be swaying to and fro as if they were torn from their foundations. Outside, on the other hand, there was the danger of falling pumice stones, even though these were light and porous; however, after comparing the risks they chose the latter. In my uncle's case one reason outweighed the other, but for the others it was a choice of fears. As a protection against falling objects they put pillows on their heads tied down with cloths.

Elsewhere there was daylight by this time, but they were still in darkness, blacker and denser than any ordinary night, which they relieved by lighting torches and various kinds of lamps. My uncle decided to go down to the shore and investigate on the spot the possibility of any escape by sea, but he found the waves

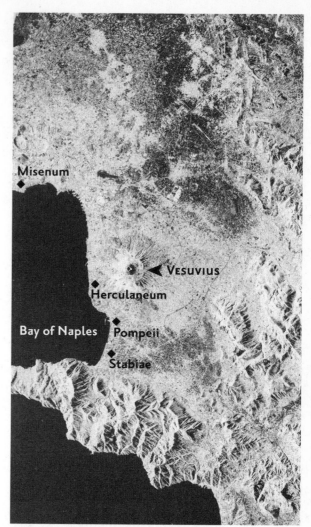

Mount Vesuvius as seen from space

still wild and dangerous. A sheet was spread on the ground for him to lie down, and he repeatedly asked for cold water to drink.

Then the flames and smell of sulfur which gave warning of the approaching fire drove the others to take flight and roused him to stand up. He stood leaning on two slaves and then suddenly collapsed, I imagine because the dense fumes choked his breathing by blocking his windpipe which was constitutionally weak and narrow and often inflamed. When daylight returned on the 26th—two days after the last day he had seen—his body was found intact and uninjured, still fully clothed and looking more like sleep than death.

Nonfiction Passages With Graphic Organizers for Independent Practice

What's Buried at Pompeii?

Fill in the circle next to the correct answer.

1. What happened to Pliny the Elder after Mount Vesuvius erupted?

   (A) He wrote letters to friends documenting what happened.

   (B) He saved citizens escaping the destruction.

   (C) He sailed to the city and rescued thousands of people.

   (D) He choked to death as a result of the flames and fumes.

2. What was Pompeii?

   (A) a volcano in Italy

   (B) an early name for Rome

   (C) a city in ancient Rome

   (D) the wife of a Roman soldier

3. How have we learned about Pompeii?

   (A) letters from Pliny the Elder and excavations

   (B) old video documenting the destruction

   (C) photographs and art from ancient Rome

   (D) ancient letters and recent excavations

4. Which of the following is <u>not</u> true?

   (A) Pompeii had about 20,000 people when it was destroyed.

   (B) Vesuvius has never erupted since the Pompeii destruction.

   (C) Herculaneum was located closer to the sea than Vesuvius.

   (D) Pliny the Younger died around the age of 52.

5. <u>Underline</u> sentences from the letters that tell about Pliny the Elder's character.

What's Buried at Pompeii?

Write a letter to a friend describing what happened to Pliny the Elder while Mount Vesuvius was erupting. Use Pliny the Younger's letter as a model by summarizing what he wrote.

![Writing icon] **WRITING** Go to www.eyewitnesstohistory.com to learn about other important events in the ancient world. Download interesting articles to share with your classmates.

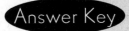

Living on a Jet Plane
page 10
1. c; 2. a; 3. d
4. Metal is waterproof. Aluminum never rusts. Storms can't damage the strong body. A plane weighs more that most houses, so it won't blow over.
5. Answers will vary.

Suited for Survival: What's on a Space Suit?
page 13
1. c; 2. d; 3. b; 4. d
5. Circle: tether, safety tether, jet pack; underline headlights, mirror, trash holder.

Dino-mite Discoveries
page 16
1. c; 2. b; 3. d; 4. b
5. Answers should include three facts from the article.

Robot Coming Through
page 19
1. c; 2. c; 3. d
4. ASIMO has arms and legs. It can walk up and down stairs. It can change direction so that it won't bump into things. It is programmed to recognize people and greet them. It recognizes and responds to its name. It waves when waved to.
5. Answers will vary.

His Place in History: Ben Franklin
page 22
1. d; 2. b; 3. d; 4. c
5. Answers will vary.

A Dog's Life
page 25
1. c; 2. d; 3. c; 4. b
5. Underline: Dogs are born with a remarkable ability to read people, making a human-dog relationship very natural. Circle key sentences under "When and Where."

Freedom's Trail
page 29
1. b; 2. c; 3. d; 4. d
5. Answers should include: escaped on the Underground Railroad, used disguises, shipped in a box.

From Sea to Shining Sea: The United States
page 33
1. c; 2. d; 3. a; 4. b
5. New Orleans

Hope for Orangutans
page 37
1. c; 2. a; 3. b; 4. c
5. (See paragraph 2 under Disappearing Act) Habitat loss, due to forest clearing . . .; forests where orangutans live . . . are being destroyed for lumber.

Get a Kick Out of Martial Arts
page 40
1. c; 2. d; 3. b; 4. d
5. Underline: kung fu, judo, t'ai chi, karate, tae kwan do.

I Was a Scientist in the Rain Forest!
page 45
1. c; 2. b; 3. c; 4. d
5. She kept a journal, observed their habitats, recorded their sounds, counted them, and photographed them.

Calling America Home
page 48
1. Answers may include: freedom, better education, to escape war, to live in safety, to be able to work, to be able to go to school.
2. Van
3. family members, friends, and relatives
4. They couldn't speak English, they didn't have any friends, things were different from what they were used to.
5. Answers may include the following ideas: They speak the same language, have similar cultures and customs, may have known each other in

their homelands, understand the difficulties of moving to a new homeland, can better help each other.

Heart Thumping Workouts
page 52
1. d; 2. b; 3. a; 4. b; 5. d

From Pampas to Patagonia: South America
page 56
1. d; 2. a; 3. b; 4. d
5. Uruguay, Argentina, Patagonia

Beastly Bugs or Cool Critters?
page 60
1. d; 2. c; 3. b
4. 2; 8; no; no; no

Sequoyah and the Cherokee
page 65
1. c; 2. a; 3. a; 4. b
5. Answers may include: They could record their history and experiences for future generations. They could communicate with each other even if they didn't live in the same place. They could spread their ideas in books, newspapers, and letters.

Nancy Ward: Revolutionary War Leader
page 69
1. d; 2. d; 3. c; 4. c
5. Answers should include three facts from the article.

Change of Heart
page 73
1. b; 2. c; 3. c; 4. d
5. Circle: hummingbird, groundhog, and humpback whale
Underline: Survival Tip for each animal

Nature's Neat Noses
page 77
1. d; 2. b; 3. a; 4. c
5. Answers will reflect each student's personal preferences.

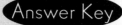

Twister!
page 81
1. c; 2. b; 3. c; 4. d
5. Students should circle the tornado safety tips.

It's About Time! Women's Rights
page 85
1. c; 2. d; 3. c; 4. c
5. Underline one key sentence related to each date in the time line.

Landslide Disaster!
page 90
1. d; 2. c; 3. b; 4. b
5. Answers may include: houses may be destroyed, roads may be covered, people may be killed, and fires may start.

Biddy Mason
page 94
1. b
2. d
3. b
4. generous, determined, businesswoman, caring
5. Answers may include: in 1947, four years later, In 1856, ten years after gaining her freedom, almost a hundred years later, November 16, 1989.

Mister Mom
page 98
1. b; 2. c; 3. c; 4. d
5. Underline one key sentence in each section. Answers will vary regarding human fathers.

Monarchs Take Flight
page 102
1. a; 2. d; 3. b
4. Answers may include: every fall, in September and October, in March, as winter ends, over the summer.
5. Answers will vary.

Celebrate Hispanic Heritage
page 107
1. c; 2. c; 3. d; 4. c
5. Answers will vary, but should be supported.

Drip, Drop, Drip! The Water Cycle
page 111
1. a; 2. b; 3. c; 4. d
5. 85% of the earth is covered by oceans and seas.

Breaking Barriers
page 115
1. c; 2. a; 3. a; 4. b
5. Rickey knew that a black player would be facing racist crowds. It would take courage and self-control for that player not to lose his temper and shout back at them.

At the Bottom of the World
page 120
1. c; 2. d; 3. c; 4. d

What's Buried at Pompeii?
page 125
1. d; 2. c; 3. d; 4. b
5. Answers may include the sentences that begin: My uncle's scholarly acumen . . . ; He changed his plans . . . ; He hurried to the place . . . ; He was entirely fearless . . . ; For a moment . . . ; After his bath . . . .